Edge of the Kingdom

Edge of the Kingdom

A Mind and Heart Altering Interactive Novel
(about the nature of God that I discovered
for myself through using marijuana)

By will I AM… (a Sky) Walker
*…who is also a SHE… at the end… you'll see ☺

William Walker

Rev. date: 04/20/2017

To order additional copies of this book, contact:
Xlibris
1-888-795-4274
www.Xlibris.com
Orders@Xlibris.com
760342

CONTENTS

AUTHOR'S NOTE
(IN THE BEGINNING ;)

I want to share an experience I had with you that has truly transformed my life. It helped me transform from an Agnostic who didn't believe in God to a "reborn" without a doubt believer. This experience has given my life true meaning and though I have fallen on some economic hardship recently, I have never been happier and more hopeful for the future. For the first time in my life, I feel completely free and ALIVE!

(think: I AM (is) Reigniting (MvM) my consciousness... And I have to admit... I just found out not long ago, that I have what psych doctors would call a mental illness... I AM (is) bipolar (with delusions)... now I don't want to offend anybody with anything I say in this book... just giving a disclaimer that absolves ME... aka Bill... Billy... William E. ... of anything that violates P.olitical C.orrectness from the entire spectrum, ranging from the anarchist liberal to the fascist conservative... I AM (is) just a bipolar stoner that writes poetic musical codes... so I call myself the Code Righter... because I can see the right codes... in everything now... because I keep getting higher and touching the fire that is my consciousness... to a more divine level... so please don't be offended by anything that I write that goes against what you believe in... it's just another version of consciousness. Like Bill Maher, who might just enjoy this God like (hidden) code when he is up in the sky... tuning in... to that Grapevine... tied to that valentine... cloaked with the power of Kings.... and the missing part... is meant to foil you... with time... ;)

This story I wrote will help give you a "taste" of what I experienced over a period of several months. And maybe I can help you transform your life into something better. If you don't believe in God, maybe I can help you find God. If you do believe in God, maybe I can help you strengthen that belief. And if we join together as One, we can reshape the world into something better. A world we can all prosper in... where no one gets left behind... where there is no rapture... or we can create the polar opposite... we all get raptured.

And if you want to make this experience as real as possible...try my suggestions. So, when you see *(parentheses with words in bold italics)*, that is an action you can **choose** to perform... like the one above where I tell you to *think or imagine*. K?... and if you are not good with codes...that is code for Ok? ☺

There is also a good tip on how to understand my writing style at the beginning of ch. 4... especially if you don't want to follow the most important instruction, where you use marijuana to hear and see all my codes.

Now, obviously, you can **choose** to read the novel how you want to, buuuttt... following these actions will really help you better understand the meaning behind this book – trust me ☺

I also wanted to make the book feel more like a movie and Make *it better* and take it Beyond its *limits* from both Silver *ends*. I'm sure many of you have read a book only to be disappointed by the movie version. The nice thing about movies is they can give you visual details that your mind may struggle with when it imagines the words. Now, I can't help with the visual (that's up to your imagination), but movies can make the story really come alive through adding music, which captivates us emotionally.

So, the first thing I would recommend is to have your phone set to a music provider like Spotify, which is what I use. Now at certain points, I will recommend you listen to a specific type of song, but you will have to **_choose_** to do it. In my first draft of this novel, I chose all the songs for you, but I realized that was a mistake. Those songs were from my playlist and only really mean something to me. And that is a key to making this little experiment a success... listening to music that means something to you. I will just give you a little descriptor of what I was listening to when I wrote the words.

Another thing I did when I first wrote the story, is I tried to imagine what the characters would look like based on actors that would be good for the role if this were a movie. I realized this is a mistake, because your mind needs to believe the characters you are creating from the words.

Now here is the fun part of imagination... I typically like to assume a role myself when I watch a movie or read a book. It helps me connect with the characters through empathy and brings the story to life in my mind. And I would bet that most of you do the same thing, though you probably don't consciously think about it. So, there are basically two main characters in my novel (male and female) and you can imagine that they are you. Be either one if you choose, because it doesn't really matter which gender they are to you... they are a reflection of God.. and that is what you are. So, dream away and I will try to describe them so you can see them very clearly in your mind.

The last thing that would really help, is if you have the desire and ability to smoke marijuana – especially when you get to the beginning of Ch. 4. Why?... because marijuana intensifies experiences and that is how my "rebirth" into faith happened. Do you have to do this? No... and I believe you will still have a mild transformation if you listen to the musical words with your heart. It just might be harder to see, or it will be less intense. This is ultimately your choice. Now... I am **_NOT_** encouraging kids to do this! I believe you should be 21 and over. And I am **_NOT_** encouraging you to break the law *(think: what a dumb law marijuana prohibition is!... but I don't want to digress...)* so smoke at your own risk... who knows if Jeff Sessions is watching you through your microwave... ☺

And I will pray that you will do nothing that could be harmful to yourself or anyone else. *(think: though marijuana doesn't make you violent... I just want to make sure to remind you... DO NOT TAKE ANY RISKS – for example – DON'T think you can fly and jump off of a building – it will never work – even though when you get really high you might believe you can – the law of gravity will NOT allow it... remember you are only high and NOT a superhero! Be SMART! Do this in the comfort and safety of your own home. AND I AM NOT KIDDING ABOUT THIS... I AM TRYING TO GET YOU TO FEEL GOD ON THE INSIDE... NOT PHYSICALLY BECOME GOD ON THE OUTSIDE... ;)*

One last thing... try not to let the three dots bother you... it just means to pause a little. I know it's not the best way to write English, but it feels right when I write this way (especially when I am high). It allows me to gather all the thoughts that are rapidly running through my mind... so the dots slow me down a little and hopefully give some understanding of what I am trying to say. And try not to mind the weird grammar (capitalization, *italics*, etc.), I told the publishing company not to edit for mistakes... this a code I'm writing... I'm talking like *(think of Yoda a lot)*... and most of you know he wasn't very good with grammar... but he was a cool kind of crazy, so you know he didn't care about using proper English... you just knew the little green dude was wicked smart (wise)... and that's all that matters. Yoda is like an Aghori *(think: like the ones from India that can be pretty crazy... but realize it is all an act... just like when you first met Yoda... but then he came down so that Luke could understand him... like the Aghori in the Believer show that only eats honey... and thinks he's Mr. Mandelbaum... and Reza is Jerry... the whole trinity of them that end up in the hospital for trying to lift too much weight.)*

So Let's Begin... *(Imagine you are in Virginia Beach, Virginia on a mild winter night and start a song on your playlist that gets the engine that is in your mind ... to slowly rev you up... like a hot motor cycle after its been idling for a few seconds... like it is about ready to have* Sex *in the 4ᵗʰ dimension... and blow your mind. So slowly turn the throttle down towards Hell (a* Kind *of Zero) and hear it wake up... think of yawning* Om *and climax to a loud roar).*

INTRODUCTION – THE DREAM IS SOOO... REAL

You see a blank sheet of perfectly white paper on a table and what looks like a female hand holding a pencil. You can see other colored pencils in the upper left hand corner of the paper resting together in the same direction. Your eyes also sense that there is smoke hovering around the paper and you realize there must be a cigarette burning nearby. The hand starts moving slowly but as time goes on, it starts to move very quickly (almost as if it is vibrating). Then your mind moves in quickly to where your perception is very close to the where the image is being drawn. This "close up" turns everything pure black and you can't see the image that is being rapidly sculpted by the high vibrational hand. So... your mind slowly decides to expand outward at a turtle's pace moving your perception further away from the paper and now you can start to see the image more clearly. The hand seems to be drawing the image of a perfectly dark circle. Then, the hand reaches for other colored pencils and starts to draw around the dark circle, and you realize it is the beginning of an eye. It is the image of an iris with vibrant colors that are mingled together. The eye is a little hard to see because of the smoke passing by the image. As the smoke meanders around the eye that slowly comes into clear view... your mind keeps panning outward to the point where you can now see both eyes and the top part of a nose with more smoke hovering about.

You can now sense that these are the eyes of a man and are showing some sort of anticipation as his cigarette and closed lipped smile comes into view. It is an anticipation in his mind of what is yet to come. It seems as if it is a fleeting moment of pure ecstasy, as the shimmering eyes show an excitement... an excitement that is created when the mind... for a brief moment of time, and feels this complete connection with your opposite polarity. Your exact opposite... and from one end you hate it... but on the other end... you love it... because it is pure ecstasy!

As your mind continues to move away from the page, you now see the hand drawn outline of a man's face start to come alive as more color is added. The fast motion of the drawing hand is starting to make your brain believe the image, and thus this story is coming alive... but you know it's just a dream.

But this dream feels sooo... real because that's how dreams feel... they feel real... especially nightmares! And you know you have no control over these... so you are afraid of them. You are afraid because you are doing something awful, or something awful is being done to you, and you can't seem to stop it. But since you have consciousness, you know you can wake up... or better stated... be reborn. You know you can turn these awful dreams into dreams full of awe. And the method is simple, as you can create an awe-full dream by keeping your eyes open and construct a day dream that is straight from level 7-11... aka heaven... but you know that pure heaven doesn't come until level 12 (which is Almighty God by the way). But eventually, you get bored at 7-11 with saving the world from Armageddon (like Bruce Willis) all the time and want to come back to reality... down to earth (level 6)... where you experience a little or a lot of hell (levels 5-0) . It's definitely scarier on earth... but when you pull off even the smallest miracles... it's exhilarating!"

(Say to yourself: and it's worth it... because it was real... because you had to take a risk... possibly even risk it all... gamble like you've never gambled in your life... and your life might have even depended on it... but when you hit the jackpot... by pulling off the impossible... and you truly save the world... you can create a heaven on earth!)

Dream or not...it feels real. Dreams are real in our minds (consciousness). And since the invisible laws of quantum physics allow consciousness to control waves and particles... our minds can control our reality... it can control what dreams we want to experience. We have a choice...it's called free will...or what our soldiers have all died for... freedom. We can choose what we want... to live in heaven??? Or to live in hell... or maybe a little of both?? I don't know about you... I'm going with heaven... cause I can't imagine being in hell with the Devil and all those insane souls that do all those horrible things to beautiful angels.

Your voice starts to slowly drift away into silence and you can hear it speaking to you... "So what's it gonna be??? The blue pill or the red pill?"

And if you are like Neo (from the movie trilogy – *The Matrix*) and want to continue and see how deep the *rabbit (in the* Headlights) hole goes... *(think: you will pick the red pill... and continue reading...).*

CH. 1 – THE DANCE...
OF DESTINY

You now see his face clearly; he is a beautiful soul and you can tell his heart is made of gold. The light inside his shell tells you he would sacrifice that heart of gold in a red-blooded heartbeat to save his brother on the battlefield. He is very respectful of authority and always follows the accepted rules. He likes being part of a well-oiled machine that purrs like that engine on that motorcycle you pictured in the beginning. The only thing with that... is he has a blind spot in seeing, the destructive nature of that beast that is purring, and destroying the earth with the carbon devil. Now, he is also a curious soul... wants to have some understanding of this world... so he is always questioning... what doesn't seem right in his particular universe... his alternate universe that lights up only his mind.

He is wearing a black leather jacket with a nice black button down, with dark jeans and a nice pair of black boots. The cigarette he is smoking is getting pretty short and that is why the smoke is snaking up to his eyes as he thinks about what is going to happen later. His concentration is so focused on the music that is playing through his headphones, he doesn't even blink as the smoke dances like a stripper on stage around his eyes.

He is leaning on his Ducati, partially sitting on the motorcycle seat with his feet to the side and his arms crossed. He waits outside a gentlemen's club on a mild winter evening *(think: it will be March 7, 2017 by the time you reach the part where I write about Omega... and these words I just wrote too)*, just after a short but soothing rain coated the parking lot and now is shimmering the yellow lights from the building. And while he is in day dreamland just after dusk... an older Mustang probably from the 90's... with a souped-up rumble, drives up playing obnoxiously loud music *(you can imagine the possible tune that these good ole country boys would be listening to – think Waylon Jennings... ;)*. And in the car, are two guys yelling out the window (like Bo and Luke Duke hooting and hollering as they jump across a bridge) as they see their buddy in the parking lot. But even this doesn't break his concentration, as he is so entrenched in his fantasy... and he is determined to play it out to where he is completely satisfied.

1

So, after they park a few stalls away… Dale and George… old high school friends of JC (aka Jack), get out of the car and put on their hats. Dale (the driver) has a black cowboy hat that closely matches his hair color and accentuates his cleanly shaven face. He wore a black sport coat, dark blue shirt, dark blue jeans, and black boots. George who is a little more outlandish than his compadre; was wearing an off-white cowboy hat that covered up his clean-shaven head, but it seems to make his thick goatee stand out more. He is wearing a button-down shirt that closely matches his hat, his jeans are lighter than Dale's, and he has them tucked into his brown boots.

They walked up to where Jack is parked. They were stumbling a little because they had already started the party earlier (at Dale's house) and the parking lot was also a little slippery from the rain that passed by about an hour ago. They get to where their friend is intensely gazed into what looks like a conscious coma, leaning on his Ducati… listening to something on his playlist… and the cigarette nub looks as if it is about to inflict permanent damage to the right nostril. Dale walks up and slowly waves his hand in front of his face to coax him back to this universe. He looks back at George and says: "looks like Jack is already imagining a little bit of heaven, has gone crazy, and has lost his ability to speak."

Slowly but surely, Jack finds his way back to this reality and the small grin that he had earlier grows around the cigarette which is just about at the nub stage. He takes the cigarette out of his mouth and flicks it on the ground. Then he reaches up to his head and pulls out his black wireless headphones *(stop your music now)*… and he is now hearing *(start imagining)* a techno beat coming from inside the club. He slowly puts the headphones in his pocket, then he takes a quick jab at Dales face, stopping within an inch of his nose, but making Dale flinch…and says "made you flinch cowboy." They all break into a big laugh and give bro-hugs where they clasp each other's hand by the thumbs and wrap the other around arm around the back. Dale also says the customary "how's it going dude, glad ya made it!"

George steps back a little and says "you need to stop smoking those dirty smelling cigarettes and start smoking something with a little kick!" as he simultaneously pulls out a small, tightly rolled, joint.

Jack laughs a little and reminds George, "you know I've never touched that stuff."

"One day buddy!" George tilts his head to the side and squints his eyes… *(think: Bill Burr impersonating former President George W. Bush)*… "we're gonna git ya!" And then gives a little wink at Jack.

Dale then puts his hand on Jack's shoulder and with a nice smile says… "are you ready to see a real Goddess in the flesh for your first time at a strip club?"

Jack gets a smirk on his mouth as he starts nodding his head up and down and says, "you've been texting me about her for a few weeks now."

Dale replies... "I couldn't believe my eyes when I first saw her... she just started a couple of months ago and I knew you would have a little pre-deployment leave, so I had to get you to see her at least once before you went back. Shit... If I weren't married, I be coming in here every Friday night until I got a date with her. Though George is single, he's too ugly and stupid to ever have a chance with her. I'm hoping she notices your rugged, but loveable looks, falls in love, and then I can live vicariously through you with the morning after stories."

Jack smiles and says... "You know I don't kiss and tell."

"Still the mama's boy goody two shoes I see," Dale replies.

Jack and Dale turn towards the entrance and start walking, while George expresses in a slightly nervous voice... "I'll be a minute...gotta get my wings so I can see the one and only Trinity up close. Save me a good seat assholes!" As he walks over to a dark corner of the building and lights up.

As they walk up to entrance you can really hear the beat coming from inside the windowless building with lots of neon lights. The techno beat that was faint when they first met half way back in the parking lot, was now loud. This techno beat ends and you hear the growl of a Harley Davidson starting up and behind is the roar of the electric guitar. Then the beat of the bass drum kicks in and it's pretty loud. It makes you feel like you are right next to the drums when the patrons start chanting "Girls, Girls, Girls..."

After the bouncers check their IDs and take their cover charge, Jack and Dale stroll into the main area where they can barely see the stage from the haze of smoke that was in the room. But where the stage is brightest, there are four angels of light. Almost topless dancers...with small pasties on their nipples and wearing skimpy thong bikini bottoms. They are moving around like they are making love to the audience... like it was each person's special night.

This was a relatively small establishment that didn't go fully nude because ownership was worried that they might not get a liquor license from the local authorities if they went fully nude.

Wrapped around the stage were a bunch of 3 foot stools and behind them were small round tables with regular chairs. There were a few women and an array of men sitting in the main stage area. There patrons were a mixed variety; from old to young, wealthy to not so wealthy, and a few different races. About half were smoking some form of cigarette or vaporizer, but not one of them said a word as their eyes were locked on the ladies and their minds were living out the fantasy of a lifetime.

Dale shouts over the music, "What time do you have to be back on base tomorrow?" as he pulls out a thick money clip from inside his jacket pocket.

They luckily find an open table right in front of the stage behind the stools that give the patrons the closest possible view. As they sit down, Jack yells back, "my pre-deployment leave ends at 1200 hrs."

Dale smiles at Jack…"Good, so you can stay out with us at least until midnight or did your strict parents give you a curfew?" He pauses a little, then adds… "and did you bring plenty of money so you can tip the lovely ladies?"

In a somewhat smug voice, Jack responds, "Curfew?… I'm on leave, not lockdown… and you know I don't throw away money on strippers. I can't stand paying for something that I can get for free. Plus, they are just a tease. It's not like they are going to go home with ya… they only make you think you have a shot so they can reach into that wallet. Then you go home all hot and bothered and you have to crack one off so you can go to sleep."

"Or do what I do and substitute my wife into the fantasy!" Then Dale with a more concerned tone, "hey… you need to loosen up a little and enjoy this… you are heading back to hell soon and could use a fantasy to ease your fall into that abyss they call the Middle East. And realize this my friend…the world can run imperfectly… and yes…I'm sure every patron in here knows the charade, but they don't care…they are getting a fantasy fulfilled…and if it is real in their minds even for only a few minutes…then I guess for some the money is worth it…like me."

Dale then kicks back in his chair a little, slaps Jack in the shoulder with the back of his hand, "I'm gonna personally sponsor a dance with Trinity for ya… she's the most expensive girl here for a private dance. But you can stay for as many songs as you want…within reason," then gives him a little wink.

They turn their attention to the stage and enjoy the rest of the show with the 4 ladies. A waitress wearing a skimpy outfit takes their order of 3 bottles of beer.

A couple of minutes later, George hurriedly walks up to the table, grabs a chair and flips it around and chimes in, "woooo boys, I'm feeling good now… got my wings… and ready to fly away with Trinity. And I just talked to the DJ and he says she is up next on the stage…the timing couldn't be any better!"

Just at that moment, the crew (that everyone considers a motley party of four) start to fade out and exit the stage one by one… with just a small covering of darkness… to hide their perfect wings from behind… as they fade through the dark curtains, that shut off the fantasy in every patron's mind.

The waitress also returns with the drinks and asks if they are going to start a tab. Dale nods and then smiles at Jack, "George and I got ya tonight, so relax and enjoy your last night of freedom."

When the stage is clear, the lights dim to where you can only see tiny lights that shine like stars in the wilderness. The fake smoke starts to slowly pour out from vents, like a volcano that is slowly releasing Hell…but in this case, it is heavenly. And you can feel the anticipation in the air as everyone's eyes in the club start to salivate…for her.

The DJ starts her song that is a mix that reminds the straight ladies (and the other side of the plate dudes) of that young dark Latin lover who kept singing about Tonight... The start of the song is all about you. *(Start a song in your headphones that reminds you of a sensual, erotic, and Loving relationship You had - then hit play).* Then with a building voice...the DJ announces, "and please welcome to the stage...the Goddess of love...the ONE and only....Trinity!!

Then as his voice abruptly ends...you hear the hint of a breeze in the song and then the beat starts to pound at your ears. The lights rise up to a perfect level to see her in all her beauty. She is standing with her head down and her arms out holding a feather boa that is draped all the way across her wingspan. She looks like an angel with her wings spread. Then when the song hits the part that make the patrons want her. And the deep drums that sound like a war beat from an ancient civilization about to attack its enemy. She whips her arms and the silver feather boa down, throws her head up, opens her eyes, and quickly, aggressively, and in a sensual way, walks down to the front of the stage.

She is wearing an outfit that seems to make her glow like a silver and gold angel in the dark. She has beautiful hair with waves that could have only come from the ocean. The light inside her body makes her skin shine even more and her face is sculpted with light of a halo that is coming from her enlightened brain. Her eyes were a dark tint but with an electric hue that you would find in an evening sky just before the darkness completely consumes all colors. Her eyes seem to sparkle even more due to a hint of glitter on her face and the soft layer of silver eye shadow. And her body had the light that says... I don't care what the shell looks like... my light blinds you and can make you see just how beautiful I am. Altogether...she was an immaculate perception for the eyes to see.

As the song progresses, she moves around the stage teasing the audience with the body movement that only a seasoned dancer could make. Then, as she returns back to the front of the stage, she happens to lock on to Jack's eyes and they are both captivated by the beauty they see. And when the song gets to the first refrain...they simultaneously and seductively mouth the words... "I'm loving you" to each other.

Immediately, Dale and George snap their heads towards Jack and their eyes open as wide as can be, accompanied by a smile of amazement at this incredible gesture she made toward their friend. They were also totally unaware that he mouthed the same words back to her in perfect unison, which might have fired them up even more.

She then starts moving around the stage again giving the entire audience the view of every angle of light coming from her body. And now begins the removing of her clothing...starting with the top. That silver and gold covering dropping to the ground... revealing her shimmering breasts. But hiding her true nature were two small silver stars.

The song is now getting to the part where that cool looking wrapper starts coming undone. She moves her head towards Jack and locks onto his soul again when she wraps her eyes around his... the message is clearly sent... "tonight... I want… to fall in love with you." She doesn't mouth the words this time but the look is enough to send the message to Jack. And he sends the same message back to her in silent fashion. Now Dale and George look at each other with more surprise, realizing there is an instant connection between these two.

As the undone wrapper part of the song continues, she slowly turns her back to the front of the stage, spreads her legs into a straight open scissors pose and lowers her back to accentuate the curvature of her lower half. She starts shaking her backside when the wrapper hits the floor after ripping off her miniskirt. And this causes the patrons to start breathing very fast, or what many call "the pants."

It is plainly obvious why she is the premier act at this club as not only is she a sight of beautiful light, but it's more about the presence she permeates. She gives off a presence that expresses pure ecstasy, one which no other girl at the club can replicate. It's why she never has to go around and solicit private dances from customers… they go to her. Her mystical aura comes from the fact that she is truly a free spirit that is not controlled by anyone or anything. Even the money that most girls will take from any customer doesn't seem to impact her as she seems to control how much money and who it comes from. All of the girls there dance primarily for the money; she dances solely for the performance, which somehow is understood by the audience in a subconscious way. She has an inner intelligence that knows the world is much deeper than the fake colored paper that makes most of us sell our souls to the devil. Her performance gives the feeling of a sacred dance that ancient cultures would do to please the Gods and Goddesses…the Goddess of love…sensuality…sex…life.

The last minute of the song, she goes around and accepts the donations from the patrons that express their gratitude for her performance. It is also a way for them to get close to her and feel the energy she exudes as they place their money in the fabric of her bikini bottom. And most of them try to get a little touch of the golden fleece that is her skin, as they deposit the money in her bikini strap. Then they walk away with a smile hoping she will accept their proposal for a private dance later in the night.

George happened to be the last patron who gave her a tip hoping he could get a one on one session later. But he knows from past experiences she is tough to get, so he tries to butter her up a little with a $20 and a nice, but simple compliment, "you are so beautiful."

As the song winds down like it began, singing with the focus on "you"… she moves to the back of the stage and strikes the same pose that she began with, but facing the opposite direction. This gives the audience one last tempting look at her apple of knowledge… and as the lights dim, she fades into the darkness from which she came from.

With that, the DJ jumps in with a soft and humble voice, "let's give the Goddess Trinity the praise she deserves."

All of the patrons start clapping, while George rises to his feet because he now has wings that he got in the parking lot for a standing ovation. He also combined his clapping with a high-pitched whistle he can make with his lips and tongue.

Jack and Dale look at each other and give a little chuckle as their friend is obviously having a good time.

Dale then asks Jack, "well...what do you think now that you've seen her in the flesh?"

"I don't say this too often to ya, but you were definitely right...she's unbelievable."

The DJ starts up the next song and the beat has a Latin flavor. He announces the next dancer while the boys continue their conversation about Trinity.

George chimes in, "unbelievable is an understatement... and dude! She was totally in to you man!"

Jack tilts his head slightly while giving a mild squint, showing a little disbelief in that statement... "I'm sure it is just part of her act and she does it to some random person each performance."

Dale leans in, "George and I have seen her enough times to know that she doesn't do that dude. She performs for the entire audience and though she may look at you and smile like she likes you... we have never seen her give that look. It's almost like you caught her off guard and provided her with something she wasn't expecting. It was like she was able to look past your eyes and see into your soul and liked what she saw. You're a good-looking dude, but I'm sure there are a lot of good-looking guys that come into this club. The look she gave you seemed to be deeper than finding you attractive on the surface."

"I'll confirm that buddy... and you know I rarely agree with Dale"

As George finishes his statement, a young dancer comes up to the table with a cute dimpled smile "how are ya all doing this evening?" While putting her hands on the shoulders of Jack and Dale, but scanning her eyes to all three of them.

"Were doing even better now that you've decided to join us" exclaims George.

"Would any of you three handsome gentleman like to join me in a private dance?" But her focus was on Jack when she asked the question hoping the best looking guy at the table would be the one who takes her up on her offer.

Jack holds up his hand, "I'm good right now," and gives her a little smile.

She turns her attention to Dale and gives him a suggestive look, "Maybe a little bit later after I catch up with my buddy that I haven't seen in a while," Dale says with a kind voice.

Finally, she directs her eyes towards George in kind of a sad puppy dog fashion.

"Shit... How can you guys say no to that face? Sure little darling... how much are we talking here?"

"$20 for a dance."

"Well, the night is early, how about we make it $15?"

She smiles and walks over to the other side of the table, reaches her hand out in a dainty fashion, and says "let's go handsome."

George grabs her hand while he stands up, looks at Dale and Jack, gives a smile and a little wink, and strolls off to the back room where the girls give you some personal attention.

As Jack turns back around from watching George with his new girlfriend (for at least a few minutes), laughs and says, "he's so high, he is going to run out of money before we are even here for one hour."

"Well, there is an ATM machine in the lobby... let's hope he has sufficient funds in his bank account to cover at least two hours." Dale laughs.

And as good timing would have it, Trinity walks out the door that leads to behind the stage with an unlit cigarette in her hand.

Dale notices her walking out that door and taps Jack on the arm. He motions with his hand for Jack to take a look as she strolls towards the back corner of the club near the bathrooms.

She has her silver bikini top back on that she delicately removed and the miniskirt that she ripped off during the performance. Even though she has covered up the most prized possessions other than her face that patrons want to see, the light she exudes still looks radiantly beautiful.

As she sits at a small table against the wall, one by one, several men and even one woman approach her and offer her a light for her cigarette. They also inquire about a private dance in the back room. And with each one of them, she sweetly declines both proposals saying that she's on a break and not quite ready to smoke her cigarette.

In the background, you can hear the next song start to play and you understand it's message... it dares you to *come and* Get what you desire... whatever *It* is...

As the song continues, Dale and Jack watch her turn down each of the offers... Dale says, "she does this all the time"

Jack looks kind of puzzled, "why...doesn't she want to make any money?"

"She doesn't care so much for the money, she knows it will come...she wants to find a situation that will turn her on. She is not your typical dancer dude and that's what makes her so appealing to everyone that comes to this club. She is the most enlightened dancer here, she's genuine and doesn't fake it for the money, thus it really turns on those she chooses to give her undivided attention to."

"What does she typically charge?"

"Depends what kind of mood she's in, but typically it starts at $50 for one dance. And if it looks like the person has a lot of money, she may double it."

"Don't you have to have a standard price for all the girls?"

No, the girls are independent businesswomen and they can haggle for whatever they think they can get. They just gotta give a cut to the owner, which is $10 for renting the private room (which typically lasts around 5 minutes), so anything over that they can keep. They just pay the cashier for the room when they leave. And they can keep all the money that they get for dancing on stage, but you have to have a choreographed performance and sign up for time slots. The most popular girls get first dibs on the best times, then it goes by seniority."

"So, George got a bargain for $15?"

"Yeah, that's the minimum price you have to pay, but we just got here and haven't been drinking much. The smartest girls with the most experience obviously make the most money. The experienced ones know not to approach you too quickly, they watch the patrons very closely and usually wait until you've got a couple of drinks in you and have been watching the stage girls for a while. Then when you're all worked up and feeling good, they move in and can get more money out of you. Now that girl with George was pretty hot, but looked a little young, so she must be relatively new and probably is a little more desperate to make some cash. They also know if they get you in the back room and can really turn you on, they can get you to stay for more than one song. And when George gets his wings, he might stay in there for 15 or 20 minutes."

Jack turns his focus back to Trinity, "She's turning down every person that is coming up to her."

"Well, based on what I saw on stage, I'm betting she's waiting for you to approach her with an offer for a private dance."

"I'm not paying $50 for 5 minutes."

"I told ya earlier I would spot your dance with her."

"That's ridiculous Dale, minus her room rental fee, that's like"... Jack pauses for a moment while he does the math... "almost $500 and hour and nobody is that good of a dancer."

"She doesn't do many private dances and everybody wants her, so its simple supply and demand. She's worth it man, and who knows...tell her you're a soldier going off to the Middle East soon to fight for her freedom to earn $500 dollars an hour. That might turn her on and she'll give you a discount."

"You mean a discount for you, because you said you got this," as he places his hand on Dale's shoulder and giving it a little shake with a sarcastic grin.

"Well, if you're going to do it, you better hurry before she accepts someone's offer. She is mostly a stage performer and only gives a few private dances per night. She sometimes takes off early too, so don't think you have all night to do this. And I know you believe in signs...this song is trying to give you one."

Right then, Dale slides $50 cash in front Jack. "Come and get it… let me know if she wants more."

Jack looks at Dale for a second with a sly look on his face, picks up the cash, slides his chair out, stands up and says "thanks man."

Dale replies in a sincere voice, "no…thank you for serving this country."

Jack looks to see if Trinity is still there and starts to walk towards the back corner. He sees Trinity sitting on a stool at the right side of a small table that is against the wall. She is now talking with one of her fellow dancers who is sitting at the left side of the table. He notices an open stool at the table in between them and that she is holding her cigarette up in the air with her right hand, as her elbow rests on the table… and it is still unlit.

When Jack gets near the back corner, Trinity and her friend see him walking up and stop their conversation. Jack stands there for a few seconds and doesn't say a word while looking at Trinity and just shifting his eyes briefly at the other girl. Normally that kind of silence makes people feel awkward, but the only person that feels awkward is the other girl and she quietly leaves the area without saying a word. Jack stands there in silence for a few more seconds while looking at Trinity's eyes, but he exudes pure confidence in this silence. And she exudes the same confidence back at him while she focuses on his eyes.

Jack then slowly looks down and reaches into his right pants pocket, pulls out his lighter and says, "looks like you need some help with the darkness." Then lights his lighter and holds it out there for her to use.

Trinity forms a coy little smile on her face, raises the cigarette to her mouth, and breathes in the darkness from the reddish orange glow Jack's lighter gives to the end of her cigarette.

She exhales, then says, "looks like you have a desire for dark things."

Jack lets the smoke pass his face, "The darkness is tempting, even to the strongest amongst us."

"So how strong are you?"

Jack pulls out his own cigarette, lights up and says, "I'm still breathing after two tours of duty in Afghanistan. So strong enough to survive hell on earth… twice…and tomorrow I'll be heading back to base to prepare for hell a third time."

"You're a soldier… you look a little older and your hair isn't as short as some of the young guns that typically come in here. You a career grunt or an officer?"

"No, I signed up a few years ago in my late 20's, just in time to get into the Marine Corps."

"So, did you come down from Quantico, or up from Jacksonville?"

"Quantico."

"And I bet you're looking for a girlfriend for one night?"

"No, I don't ever look for girlfriends, I stumble across them from time to time. I'm just here with my two buddies that I grew up with from high school.

They wanted to give me one last night of fun before I head out and see nothing but women in blue burqas for the next seven months. Plus, it gives my buddy Dale an excuse to give his wife so she doesn't get mad at him for going to a gentlemen's club." Jack turns his head back and sees Dale gazing motionless at the latest stripper on stage. George is back and seems to be doing his own little dance in the chair with bent arms up in the air and his fore fingers pointing to the sky.

Trinity takes another drag off of her cigarette, leans back to see around Jack and says, "I've seen those two in here before, they're generous tippers. Especially the one in the white hat. I believe his name is... starts with a G."

"Yeah, that's George, he gets extra generous when he smokes a little herb first."

Trinity's eyes flicker to life... "He likes to smoke pot...not a bad thing in my book."

"Well, George does it a lot; he's single and is a mechanic that owns his own shop, so no "bosses" to worry about. Dale on the other hand is married and works for a company that randomly drug tests, so he only does it a couple times a year in order not to get caught by his "bosses.""

"What about you soldier? Ever partake?"

"Never." As Jack smoothly glides over to the stool and takes a seat.

"Why not? Afraid of Uncle Sam or the local cops coming down on ya?"

"Not my thing, I like being in control of my mind and body...so I don't do drugs."

"Well, I saw you sipping on a beer when I was on stage...you do understand that alcohol is a drug?"

"That's different... first of all, it's legal. Second, I can control the intake and keep tabs on my sobriety. And third..." he takes a nice smooth drag from his cigarette, then blowing the smoke out of the left side of his mouth, smiles and says, "I don't want to ruin my health with that shit." Then he gives a little wink and a confident sexy smile that would make most women's knees buckle.

Trinity belches out "Ha", then starts to laugh in mild disbelief... "you are a smooth talker Corporal Cool."

"Corporal Cool huh... I've had some nicknames throughout my life, but not one as creative as that."

"Well, I'm known for my creativity, but sometimes it gets me in trouble."

"I can see that in the way you dance... So, what creative thought made you decide on the nickname Trinity?"

"You don't think that's my real name?"

"Well, you look and act like you are in your early 30's like me, so I'm pretty sure your parents didn't name you after the woman in the Matrix Trilogy, which came out in the late 90's. And I'm pretty sure Trinity was not a popular name during the 80's; so unless your parents are extremely religious, you had to create that one up on your own."

"Wow, good looking, honest, and perceptive, I can see why girls stumble into being "friends" with you." As she gives air quotes with her fingers when she says friends. "I actually didn't come up with the name." She takes one last drag on her cigarette and puts it out in the ashtray as she exhales. "Got to give credit where credit is due... some guy gave it to me when he tried to pick me up in college. It was an interesting pick up line I must say. He came up to me in a bar and asked me if my name was Trinity. I said no...why? He says...because only the Oneness of God could be as perfect as you."

Jack laughed, "clever...did it work?"

"His creativity caught me at first, so I talked with him for a little while, but it fizzled out within a half an hour. Beyond that opening line, he was shallow and could only engage in random small talk...there was no depth to his soul. But I remembered the name he gave me when I started here and thought it would make for a good stage name."

"I'm sure it's pretty smart not to give out your real name here."

"Yeah, and I have a regular Uber driver to take me to and from the club so no stalkers can run my plates. Plus, it is easier to see if someone is following you when you don't have to drive yourself. And I'm not always sober enough to drive home."

"Drinking and driving can get you in trouble."

"I don't drink alcohol," she says with a wry smile on her face."

Jack smiles and takes another drag off of his cigarette. He then feels a hand pat down on his left shoulder. George steps into the conversation, "hey beautiful, if my buddy Jack doesn't want a private dance with ya, I'll be glad to take his place."

Jack looks back at Trinity and calmly responds, "don't mind my friend, he doesn't believe in foreplay and always goes in for the kill shot right away...that's why we call him minute man, cause that's all your gonna get."

George laughs, "Ahhhh, don't believe him sweetheart, it's at least two, and it will be two minutes in paradise! I was just on my way to the bathroom and wanted to make sure he doesn't talk you to death. My boy here is known to be a procrastinator and has a hard time making up his mind. Sometimes he just needs a little nudge because his brain will overthink everything. So, if he doesn't ask you for a dance soon and you're looking for a man that appreciates your true beauty, come on over to my table and I promise you that you will be well compensated for it." He then reaches out for her hand and when she obliges, he gives her knuckles a little peck.

George then turns his attention back to Jack, putting both hands on his shoulders, "my back teeth are starting to float buddy...listen, don't take too long trying to impress this beautiful goddess with your intellect; I talked Dale into getting out of here in a little while and head to a bar where I can find a woman that I have a chance with. So, get what you came for... the dance."

Jack replies with a friendly smile, "you still have your wings man?"

"Oh yeah...like a hummingbird!" Then he gives Jack's shoulders a little shake and heads off towards the bathroom.

Jack looks back at Trinity and they both start to laugh.

Trinity adds, "he's quite the character."

"Yep, he is one-of-a-kind, and with a heart of gold... He would jump in front of a truck to save your life... a true friend. So is Dale, but Dale is a lot more reserved and down to earth; what you might call typical."

Are you typical... Jack? Smiling at the revelation of his name just a minute ago, and then decides to give a little payback, "That is your name isn't it?"

Jack takes one final drag of his cigarette and puts it out in the ashtray, "actually, it's a nickname, but doesn't quite have the interesting background story behind it like yours does."

"Please enlighten me." Trinity says with a hint of sarcasm.

"Well it's an acronym and I'll reveal it when I get the real name of the cubed goddess." Jack is smiling gently with just his lips hoping she likes his wit.

"Ya know, I really like the name Jack. It reminds me of that story of how you can climb a natural green stairway to heaven and have fun with the Gods... So I'm good with Jack." With the distinct beat of the next song starting *(think – Rachel T.)*... Trinity stands up from her stool, leans over to where her lips come within a fraction of Jack's left ear and gently whispers, "would you like to Dance *with the* Devil... inside of me?"

Jack pauses... then says inquisitively, but with a touch of shyness... "How much are we talking about?"

Trinity then looks him deeply in the eyes, connecting with his soul...and with a voice filled with appreciation, "You already paid me when you decided to share your light with my darkness."

She then reaches out and softly caresses his hand until it latches onto hers, eventually lifting him out of his seat. She then gently leads the way to the private room, where personal attention to a customer's ego takes center stage. As they pass near the point of Dale and George's table, his buddies smile at Jack with the joy of knowing he will be experiencing a 5-minute taste of what the Garden of Eden might have been like. Where the greatest temptation man has ever encountered occurred. And before they lose sight of their friend; George's finger point from his left hand, that is floating in the air, slowly transforms into a thumbs-up. And with his right hand still pointing to the sky, together sends him an obvious message, as if to say... enjoy a little trip to heaven.

When they get to the private dance room, they have to pass through a dark glass door that isolates the room from the rest of the club. Jack notices that the music playing is different than what the DJ is playing in the main hall of the club and is a pre-recorded track of various songs. One of the dancers is paying the $10 rental fee for the small enclosed room she used to entertain a customer that is now walking back to the main area of the club. There are 12 small cubicle rooms, four on each side of the bouncer away from the entrance. Each cubicle room has a front wall of dark glass, so the bouncer can monitor the activities in the room, but still give them some privacy. Jack takes a quick look around and sees that seven of the rooms are occupied. Each room seems to be about 10' x 10' with a small padded chair in the middle. There is not much light in the main area of the private lounge as tiny white lights from the ceiling shine like stars on a clear night. But in each of the cubicle rooms, the light is brighter, but shines like an amber glow that you might find on the outskirts of Hell. Not the scary Hell... but the one that is sensual, tempting, and provocative. There is a small railing about half way up on each of the non-glass walls that the dancers can use to contort their bodies into unique positions. As they walk up to the table; Trinity gives a happy greeting to her fellow employees and asks for room five. The song that was playing ends and you hear the beat of a new song start up *(start playing a song that reminds you of the* 4th *Dimension - which is the emotions that you have when a friendship turns to a lustful love... that make you say... Om... g!)...*

The bouncer then escorts her and Jack to a room in the back. He politely opens the glass door for them and shuts it once they are in the room. Jack takes off his leather jacket and drapes it over the back of the chair. The sound quality in the room is quite outstanding. It almost seems as if the sound from the song is coming from nothing, like a whisper in the dark letting you know you are alive. This song has an energy which sounds like a heartbeat that is anticipating something amazing.

As Jack takes his seat, Trinity starts walking around him slowly in a sexy strut that makes the atmosphere start to drip of sensuality. And as she walks around him, she lightly drags her fingertips across his left shoulder, moving around to his upper back, then to the right shoulder. When she gets back to the front of where he is sitting, she steps away a few feet in the opposite direction. She stands there with her feet about a yard apart and her back is slightly arched to accentuate her dark backside. She slowly starts moving her hips back and forth, timing it to every other beat of the song. At the same time, she uses her hands to slowly lift her wavy ocean-like hair to the sky with the twinkling lights, then letting it slowly cascade back down to her upper back. As her hands come down from releasing her hair, she pulls the tie that keeps her bikini top attached to her neck. The top is then slowly removed and held out by her right arm and then released to the floor. Then she slowly reaches for the snaps on her mini skirt, releasing the connection, and causing the little silver cape to fall to the ground. And it seemed to fall in slow motion *(think; because the little gold strings flapped liked wings and helped it land like a butterfly with damaged feet).* Now, her delicious apple is exposed except for a tiny string going down the middle and disappearing when it covers the two small humps directly beneath her. It has a shimmering red glow from the amber lights in the room bouncing off her radiant skin. It is also noticeable that she is wearing silver glitter all over her body which is captured perfectly by the red lights. She makes his eyes bulge out towards her when her backside bulges out towards him, as her upper torso moves ever so slowly… gravitating down due to the pressure of the sound. Then when her back is about parallel with the ground, she lifts her head slightly, and snaps it back at Jack where she can look at him with just one eye. At the same time, she reaches her hands around and slaps the meaty portions of what he desires, then slowly, moving them to the top of her love heart.

She rises up, then turns around when the echoing voice is singing, walks up to Jack, and bends over to touch his outer thighs. She starts putting pressure on them to close, while at the same time looking up at his eyes through her eyebrows. Her legs are now together as her apple shaped heart of desire shakes from side to side following the beat. She slowly slides her hands to the top of his knees and her eyes are piercing so deeply into his that she can see the excitement growing in his mind. She then looks down to the are that is filling with blood and it seems to be growing quicker than what is happening in his mind. She feels her heartbeat now outpacing the music in the song and she starts moving her hands up towards the blood-filled snake in his jeans. She turns her head slightly to the side while closing her eyes. Her mouth starts to open and it seems to have a silent moan emitting from it as she breathes in his spirit. Her hands barely miss the expanding denim, eventually working their way on to his shirt. As her hands move up his shirt, she ever so slightly opens her eyes and moves her head to where her nose can barely touch his ear. Her arms now wrap around the back of his neck like an interlocking chain, while her legs straddle his horse. The glistening light coming from her breasts that are only covered by two small stars compress against his chest. She leans back ever so slightly and her body comes to a complete stop when her face moves back and locks directly in front of his.

Their eyes move in a way that makes it seem as if they are connected. They both have the same look in their eyes, the look of pure ecstasy. There seems to be a connection beyond simple lust and it is almost as if their souls were reuniting from a past life.

As the echoing voice finally fades away for good this time from the song… the beat intensifies once again… she starts pulsating her body to the beat of the song in a snake like fashion over his erect body. As their genitalia meet from the gliding back and forth movement from her snake like motion, he can't help himself and moves his hands to her upper thighs. He starts sliding them back along her golden fleeced skin until they reach the **knowledge** he so desires. His hands then apply pressure that helps intensify her movements, creating an even greater friction between their legs and genitalia. As the song progresses towards the end, they both feel a rise in their libidos and their breathing increases.

Trinity starts to feel something she has never felt in the countless dances she has provided customers in the past. She starts to feel the beginning stages of what will lead her to an ultimate climax. Part of her is afraid because this has never happened to her before, but her excitement overwhelms the fear as she realizes ...Oneness... that overwhelming connection with another being of light.

As the excitement in her body rises, she increases her movements even faster. She then can see in his eyes that he is feeling the same thing as her...no words are said...they just know it's real. He is now at his maximum growth and needs to adjust in the seat a little to help expand the cramped space in his jeans.

Finally, just before the song loses most of its beats and rhythms, it happens... the rush of pure energy fills her body. As she exhales in pulses that give a moan, it means she travelled to the edge of the Kingdom...to the edge of Heaven. Her body quivers as the song slowly winds down, her nose and forehead touch his, while her hands are cupping the back of his head. He tries to move in for a kiss by tilting his head to the side, but as his lips start to press against hers, she suddenly opens her eyes and pulls back away from him. She knows this is against club policy and the bouncer could be knocking on the glass door soon. Plus, it violates her rule to not get emotionally involved with any client. They sit there for a few seconds looking at each other while the song ends and the next one is about to begin. *(stop your music player – pick a new erotic song – then hit play again... and pause your reading a little and go off into dream heaven with the music... that God is sending... ;)*

Trinity whispers in his left ear... "you want to go one more time partner... while that stallion is still hot? I'll get it to finally break down and emit that thunder... that comes out crackling... like flaming white light ... in Roman Candle flight."

Jack smiles with his eyes on fire as the next song begins and says... "I Feel *you*... you wicked *fashion mode*... playing in the little room...screeching those tires... to that fucking tune."

Trinity fires up those stems of pure sugar cane delight... that start with the apple of the night... she strokes that stallion with the movement of her inner thighs... it starts crackling even hotter... she knows... it won't be long before it begins to explode... she starts thinking... while her breath moans out... *I know I'm in ecstasy heaven... when I can make a guy do that... over the denim... I pulled him up to level seven... with my head thrusted back... and a sexy roll ... it will release the fire... when I give it* One Touch... *and I turn up a* New Volume... *in his soul...*

Jack gets a look on his face like he knows its moments away. But instead of that look of pure ecstasy... starting the fire in that love tube... he gets this look of wide eyed anxiety... as he leaves the moment and goes to the future... he starts thinking... *this has never happened before... so quickly... and in my pants... it might seep through... and my friends will know... that I couldn't hold my load... how can I stand up when the time is real?* So he says to Trinity in a concerned tone, "I don't want this to happen here."

Trinity wakes from her state of bliss... just as she was working her way up to number two. She realizes he's afraid to let go and fly when nature says... *you're not going to stop me... with your mind games... think of baseball all you want... it's not going to prevent the dam from breaking.* So her body stops in its tracks before the end of the song. Her face loses its lift and she says in a disappointed tone... "time is up"... and she stands up from the saddle she enjoyed riding during those songs.

Jack laughs a little and in a slightly embarrassed tone and says, "I'm gonna need a minute here before I get up, I might actually hurt myself."

As she waits for Jack to simmer down a little, she puts her bikini top and mini-skirt back on. She looks out at other rooms and sees a couple of dancers performing for their clients and wonders what might be going through their minds at this moment. She knows that it is nothing like what she just experienced, because day after day, these fantasies are all about the money.

Though she always gets a tiny rush from turning on her clients, she has never experienced a full orgasm herself. Her body feels electrified, but that good feeling turns and she feels a sudden influx of pain in her gut, which eventually finds its way to her heart. The pain is knowing that after tonight she will probably never see him again... he is leaving for the Middle East soon after tomorrow.

Jack finally calms down enough to put on his jacket. They depart the room and she pays the cashier the rental fee of $10. Jack pleads with her a little, "let me at least get the room fee."

Trinity smiles in appreciation, "It's ok soldier, I kind of know what hell is like, so save it for your trip back to base tomorrow."

As they walk out of the private room, Jack smiles back and says, "thank you, and I have to say that was the most incredible 10 minutes I have ever spent with a woman fully clothed."

Trinity smiles, "Your welcome Jack, maybe you'll come visit me again when this tour of duty is over." There seemed to be sadness in her voice as she ended the sentence.

Jack could sense her sadness that their time is over and contemplates an idea that most men wouldn't have the guts to ask at this moment. But he isn't like most men...and he realizes that they made a connection. Not just a sexual one... a connection that says this person may just be part of my destiny. One that makes him feel that there just might be a higher power involved.

"When are you done tonight? Would you like to meet up at another bar later with my friends and I?"

"That sounds like fun, but I have had a long day and don't really have the energy to go bar hopping."

Jack gets a slight look of disappointment, "Ok, I understand" and quickly hides his disappointment with a small smile.

Trinity then decides to do something she has never done in the couple of months she has been dancing, "You know, I'm starving and would love to get some pancakes. Would you and your friends want to get some food before you hit the bars? I don't want to mess with your plans though, so if you don't want to...I understand."

Jacks disappointed smile quickly turns to one that electrifies his eyes, "I'm pretty sure they won't mind. When do you punch out?"

"I just did, give me a few minutes to change into something more comfortable and I'll meet you in the lobby."

"Sure, I'll let the boys know."

Jack heads back to the table as Trinity heads to the door that leads to the dressing room back stage.

When Jack arrives back at the table, George is up by the stage handing more of his hard-earned money over to a beautiful blonde, while Dale turns down another private dance offer.

"Jacko!" Dale exclaims, "how was it? Did Trinity ruin you for all other women?"

"Well, if we would have stayed for the length of a second song, she would have accomplished that goal. And by the way...here is your $50 dollars back." He slaps the money down on the table and flashes a smile that shows a touch of arrogance.

"No way! She gave you a free dance? I would've guessed that to be impossible."

George returns to the table, "Hey Jack, how was your little taste of heaven?"

"Awesome, but I have to say it was more than just an erotic dance; there was a connection that we felt too, much deeper than surface shit."

Dale jumps in, "We could sense that when she was on stage." He looks over to George, "guess what? he got a free dance!"

"No way!... Jack, you've always had the gift with ladies."

"Well, we're going to get some pancakes now too; you guys want to join us?"

"What?" George says with a little shock, "you got a free dance and now you're going on a date? You're such a lucky bastard."

"Maybe it's just good karma dude," as Jack shrugs his shoulders.

Dale laughs and says, "You got karma coming out of your ass man, and if you pull off the hat trick later tonight, I'm betting there is a few horse shoes up there too."

"Are you guys going to join us or what?"

"Well... as much as we would love to hang out with a creation from heaven, we don't want to turn your motorcycle into a 4-wheeler. Plus, in about a half an hour, I gotta be George's wingman when we troll the bars looking for his future wife."

George gets a look of surprise. "Hey, I don't need a wife, just someone to comfort me tonight when I lose my wings."

Dale smiles and looks back at Jack, "I kind of had a gut feeling this might happen tonight. Something told me that a girl that is your exact opposite might be something that could spark something in you."

George adds... "Maybe she'll even get you to stop heading back to the Middle East and fighting in a meaningless war."

Jack gives a slight eye roll, "You gotta stop smoking so much pot George, you get more liberal every time I get back from a tour."

"Hey, I just want my brother from another mother to stop risking his life for a conflict that only creates more hatred and enemies... didn't this country learn anything from Vietnam?"

"Ok Gandhi, let our boy go get some pancakes with his new love at first dance." Dale gets up and gives Jack a quick hug. "If it doesn't work out, give us a text later and you can join us out at the bars. But I gotta a feeling it will, so... luv ya man... and be safe. We want to have a barbeque on the beach with ya this fall when you return."

George walks around the table and gives Jack a hug too, "take care bro, you'll be in my prayers."

"Thanks boys, and I'm sorry for cutting on you guys so early in the night."

"Don't worry about it... No man can turn down an offer to eat pancakes with the Holy Trinity!" George busts out laughing.

Jack gives one final wave to his friends and heads towards the lobby. Though he feels a little sad and a little guilty abandoning his friends so early in the night; he feels an energy that he has never felt before...it makes him feel awake...it makes him feel... reborn.

CH. 2 – THE IGNITION...
OR FIRE IN THE BRAIN

As Jack makes his way to the lobby, the music from the club starts to muffle when the glass doors close. He's looking around, but she hasn't come out of that door that says "employees only." The time starts passing away slowly, so he lights up a cigarette to try and kill the time faster. When that cigarette is over, he starts to get a little nervous... thinking that she may have changed her mind and went out a different way. Maybe she realized that hanging out with a man you just met at a strip club who is leaving to go half way around the world, to the depths of hell, is a Wrong *decision*. That he's only looking for one thing... that thing she doesn't do with anybody that she doesn't love. Maybe the whole dancer thing is just an act? Maybe it gives her the opportunity to go to the edge of the cliff... take a peek... feel the thrill... soak in the rush... and then walk away safely.

When he looks at his watch to see that 15 minutes have gone by; she hasn't come out, he starts thinking it might be time to leave. He can't go back into the club to hang out with his buddies, because he would have to explain that he was ditched. He sees the door to the exit and pictures his hand pushing on the door, but something tells him to wait. He decides to listen to some music on his phone and pulls out his headphones. He presses the icon that provides new music to listeners each week. When he sees the first song on the list, he starts to believe it is not just a coincidence, that a message is being sent, and makes him think there is some truth to his doubts. He decides to hit the play button... *(listen to a song that reminds you of a time you almost made a* Wrong *or bad decision when it comes to love ...listen to the words to feel what is going through Jack's soul. And don't continue reading until the song over)*

When the song ends, Jack puts away his headphones and realizes that it must have been just a dream. It's been almost 20 minutes and he is not going to wait forever. Dale and George are going to be leaving soon and he doesn't want to see them while he is waiting in the lobby and possibly looking like a fool. There is an aching in his stomach as he turns toward the front door and feels as if he has already entered hell...early than he planned. Then before he gets to the exit, he hears the clicking sound that a turning doorknob makes and looks back to see a beautiful angel coming through the "employees only" door. She has transformed into something different than he saw on stage, but it is just as beautiful. Trinity emerges with her hair in a ponytail and that she lost her glow of silver and gold. She is wearing blue sweat pants and a gray sweatshirt with a large orange I in the middle with blue trim. What was truly beautiful was the relieved smile she gave when she saw him waiting for her. It's the kind of smile that made her eyes light up and he could easily peer into her soul.

"Sorry I took so long, I was worried you might leave without me. I took a quick body shower and stripped off the heavy makeup. Then as I was lightly touching up my makeup, my best friend slowed me down by telling me her latest boyfriend problems. And when you are in this line of work, you end up with a lot of boyfriend problems. She was really upset, so I tried to listen to her until she felt better."

"Don't worry about... I found a few ways to pass the time." Jack smiles, then says, "I'm gonna take a stab in the dark here and guess that you don't have a boyfriend."

"Why would you want to stab me?" Trinity giggles a little. "And you would be guessing right. If I had a boyfriend I wouldn't be getting pancakes with you right now. I just moved out here a couple of months ago and am still settling in to my new life. And I'm a little like you, I don't look for boyfriends... but they kind of run into me rather than stumble. So... are you ready to get some food? Are your friends joining us?"

"No, George needs to find a nurse later that will rub his sore feet when he lands hard from losing his wings, so they are hitting the bars in a few."

"Or he needs some comfortable shoes." She winks, then says, "let's go, I'm starving... thank God the pancake house is only a few minutes down the road from here."

Jack gets the door, "you don't have a problem riding on a motorcycle, do you?"

"Nope, as long as you don't try to impress me and drive with your eyes closed using the force."

"I haven't finished my Jedi training with Yoda yet, so you'll be safe with that. Just hold on tight, because it is slippery when wet."

As they walk through the parking lot, Jack takes his jacket off, "why don't you wear this, it will keep the breeze off you better."

She gives him a smile that says "thank you" as they approach his Ducati. He hops on and starts up the engine, giving a nice twist of the throttle to hear her roar...*I'm alive!* Trinity gets on and wraps her arms around his chest and can soon feel the beat of his heart... making her heart feel more alive.

As they pull out of the parking lot and on to the highway, they both sense something In *the air* Tonight (**think – like an** *axel* Rudi *pell... ;).* The air feels heavy with moisture and you can see flashes of electrical light in the evening sky as another scattered thunderstorm approaches. But there is no sound of thunder… not yet. As they ride the short distance to the pancake house; Trinity looks up into the sky to see the intermittent patches of stars in the darkness that go in and out of view from the pillow like clouds. She thinks how easy it is to miss the beauty of the darkness and how people take it for granted. Probably because they are sleeping and letting the darkness recharge them with fresh electrical energy. The energy that only gets noticed when they wake up the next morning, but mistakenly giving credit to the sun for their renewed spirit. She thinks how light actually drains our energy because it convinces our consciousness to be awake and perform activities that require our energy to be drained. She smiles knowing that darkness is what gives us life…not the light.

A few minutes down the road, they pull up to the pancake house which looks like a small metal mobile home. They are able to park right in front because the restaurant is basically empty. When they walk in they notice another couple sitting in a booth talking over some coffee and a few other people at the counter looking at their phones while they eat a late-evening meal. The lone waitress working is an older African-American woman in her 50s and is talking to the cook as Jack and Trinity walk to a back-corner booth and slide into their seats. The window illuminates every so often as the lightning from the distant thunderstorm slowly approaches.

"This place is small, but they have great food." Trinity exclaims as Jack starts looking over the menu.

The waitress walks up, "well hi Trinity, you don't usually show up this early in the night; and where is the posse of dancers that usually accompanies you?" As she places two glasses of water in front of them.

"Hey Sherry, I put in a few hours, but I called it quits early tonight. I had a long day, plus I wanted to see the fire in the rain with my new friend Jack."

Jack and Sherry give a cordial hello to each other.

As Jack goes back to the menu, Sherry looks at Trinity and gives her a little smile with raised eyebrows acknowledging Jack's good looks. Then says, "Well, according to my weather app, the storm should be here in about 15 minutes and it looks like a quick one from the radar. What can I get you guys tonight?"

"I'll have the usual" says Trinity.

"Coffee and 3 buttermilk pancakes, and for you hun?

Jack takes a few more seconds looking at the menu… "I'll take the same but could you add a side of bacon to mine?"

"Sure thing sweetheart…should be only a few minutes guys," then Sherry walks away from the table.

Jack looks back at Trinity, "I'm going to take another stab in the…" he pauses and smiles, "…the light… and guess that the college you went to, where you got your holy name was University of Illinois."

Trinity's jokingly drops her mouth open, "Wow, you keep amazing me Jack with how perceptive you are... two for two." Then adds, "I earned a degree from U of I in education to teach social science."

Jack says, "A teacher... that's cool. I'm from Illinois too; did you live there or just go to school there?"

"Both, I was born in Geneva... I think... and lived in the area until I went off to college."

Jack's has a look of bewilderment... "You are not sure where you were born?"

"Well, my birth was somewhat unusual. I was abandoned as a new born and left in the Geneva train station. I guess someone notified the police and a few days later, I was adopted by a couple and they raised me in the area. So, I'm guessing it was Geneva, but there are quite a few small suburban towns in the vicinity."

"Wow, that is unusual... so do you have any clue who your birth parents are?

"No, but that is ok, I was raised by a wonderful couple and they gave me a great childhood." She then deflects. "Where in Illinois are you from Jack?"

"I grew up in Glencoe; are you familiar with it?

"Oh yeah, isn't that the town where the movie Risky Business was based."

"Yep, anybody that is familiar with iconic teen movies from the 80's recognizes the name."

"Yeah, a lot of great teen movies like the Breakfast Club, Sixteen Candles, Ferris Bueller's Day Off, are from the 80's and based in Chicago. She then reaches into her purse and pulls out her sunglasses, puts them on and says, "looks like University of Illinois!" She then gives a wide gaping smile like Tom Cruise did in the movie Risky Business.

Jack laughs... "I remember that part in the movie, where Tom Cruise's character is being interviewed at his house to get into Princeton. And at the same time, he is hosting a brothel party while his parents are on vacation. It eventually turns into a *tangerine* Dream where they make Love *on a real* Train..."

Sherry returns with their coffee mildly disrupting their conversation. After she leaves, Jack decides to change gears and ask an obvious but somewhat difficult question. "So... you went to college in Illinois to be a teacher and you end up in Virginia working at a gentlemen's club?"

"Gentlemen's club... very PC Jack, most people around here call it a strip club." Trinity then takes a short deep breath, "Well... after college, I landed a job as a high school teacher in the suburbs of Chicago. I taught mostly World Geography, but dabbled in other subjects like U.S. History, Psychology, and Current Issues. Things were going pretty well until I met God a few months ago and wrote an online book about the experience." She pauses to see how he reacts to that statement. There wasn't much of a reaction, so she continued. "Then I resigned my teaching position when the risk I took with the book caused some controversy. I needed to find work, so I called my best friend from college who lives out here with her boyfriend. She's the one who held me up a little at the club when you were waiting in the lobby. She started dancing on the side to help her pay off her college debt and when her degree didn't help her get a job, she became a full-time dancer. When I told her about my resignation and that I wanted to pursue a career writing; she said I could make some great money dancing while I write a new book about God. So, I did what Tom Cruise did in *Risky Business*; I said *what the fuck* and moved out here."

Jack's look of bewilderment returns. "So, you're telling me that a book about God caused you to resign your job as a teacher. I'm not sure how that is possible unless you were trying to preach to kids in a public school."

"No, it wasn't the book that created the biggest controversy. Though it had some swearing and sexual references, I didn't mention anything in my book to my students. I did do a few things that ruffled some feathers, but the biggest controversy started when I admitted in a blog post how I met God."

"And how exactly did you meet God?" Jack asks with a tone of curiosity.

"I smoked marijuana one Friday night and had an experience that can only be described as truly divine. And every time I smoked after that, the experiences became more intense with visions about the nature of God. They even continued when I wasn't smoking, which made me realize that it wasn't just a drug-induced hallucination. This overall experience transformed my life in such a positive and dramatic way that I felt I had to write a book about it. I wanted to share my experiences with the world, hoping it might help others find God too. But with sharing my experiences, I had to be honest about how I found God. So, I wrote in a blog post that marijuana was the key; and I also advocated that states who were voting to legalize it in this past election, get out the vote and pass their resolutions. This obviously didn't sit well with the school because it is an illegal activity in Illinois, unless you have a medical issue. Now I understand that being a teacher means you are also a role model and you shouldn't endorse an illegal activity; even if you believe that the law is ridiculous. So, my admission and support of marijuana created so much tension that I ultimately decided it was in the best interest of everyone involved that I resign my teaching position."

Jack's face shows some disbelief, "now I have never smoked pot myself, but I know quite a few people who do... like George... and not one has ever claimed to have met God."

"Well, I didn't actually meet God... that's impossible. I felt like God was communicating to me by going through me... like a possession, but a good one."

Jack's face still shows disbelief as he sits there listening.

Trinity continues. "Haven't you ever heard of ancient cultures using drugs to connect with the spiritual world? One example would be religious teachers in the Amazon called Shaman using a plant-based mixture called Ayahuasca.

It contains a chemical simply known as DMT and it supposedly gives incredible hallucinations that help Shaman gain insight to spiritual knowledge. And I do recall you asking George if he still has his wings... aren't humans with wings called angels?

"Yeah, but he is just saying that he's feeling good from the drug."

"Or, he's not consciously connecting the experience to something that could be real. The problem today is most people don't believe you can directly experience God in a supernatural way. That God only directly interacted with man thousands of years ago and for some reason stopped doing that in the modern era. Billions of people around the world believe men like Abraham, Moses, Jesus, Mohammed, etc., were directly visited by God or were God; but if you claim that today, you are schizophrenic, or just plain crazy and need help. My experiences got me to believe that anyone can experience God directly if your heart and mind are open to that idea. The drugs just heighten the experience and make it feel real where it really counts... in your heart."

"Well, why don't you just go to church and experience God there?"

"You can, but there *lies* another *little* problem... organized religion. Religions are like a fleetwood *Mac* that want power and the way to get it is by convincing people that they alone have the keys to the kingdom of heaven. That only through them will you be able to reach God directly and that it is only possible after you die. And while you're on earth, you can have indirect contact only through the prayers and rituals of the faith."

"So you think religions are bad?"

"No, religions do a lot of good through charity and helping people through a community of believers. Where I feel religions go wrong is when they try to monopolize God or try to elevate their beliefs above other beliefs. This only leads to division and hatred, which will ultimately lead to violence." Trinity notices Sherry walking over with their food. "And speaking of violence... I'm going to devour these pancakes coming at us!"

Sherry lays the plates down and says, "here you go guys and do you need more coffee?"

"No but I could use some extra butter," says Trinity.

"Oops my bad, I sometimes forget that you're the butter girl. I'll go get you some sweetie."

"I'll take some more coffee if you don't mind." Jack adds.

"My pleasure handsome!" Sherry then walks back to the kitchen.

"She really likes to use terms of endearment."

Trinity smiles, "well, she's a very nice person and when you work on mostly tips, it doesn't hurt to butter people up."

Sherry returns and says, "here is some fresh butter for you and let's top that coffee cup off for ya."

They both thank her and she responds humbly, "any time."

As they start to prepare their pancakes with butter and syrup, Trinity asks Jack, "so now that you know a little of my story; why don't you tell me a little of yours?"

"Okay, you know that I'm from Glencoe for starters, but my family moved to the Virginia Beach area the summer before my freshman year of high school. I was a decent student and a decent athlete, but a little bit of a procrastinator and never really gave 100% for anything. After high school, I wanted to be a pilot in the military, so I went to community college and started taking flying lessons. I even participated in an officer training program for the Marine Corps up at Quantico for six weeks on my summer break. I didn't care for it that much because I don't like people ordering me around. Then I learned I wouldn't be flying as much as I thought, so I didn't go back the next summer to complete the training. I considered being a commercial pilot, but gave up on flying when I realized how much I hated flying in the clouds where I couldn't see and had a hard time putting faith in my instruments to guide me. So not knowing what I really wanted to do for a career, I decided to drop out of school and stop wasting money. I went into housing construction because the money was good and did that for a few years. But the market crashed and got laid off, so I got a job as a bartender and did that for a few years until I got tired of the late-night hours. Now I'm in my late 20s and I realize I haven't accomplished anything worthwhile. I was living solely for myself and had not really contributed anything of real meaning back to society. So I decided to give the military another shot and enlisted into the Marine Corps. Since I didn't have a degree or any officer training, I started at the bottom and accepted the idea of taking orders. Now that I was older, I didn't mind taking orders, because I learned that a well-oiled machine needs each part to work with other parts. I also believe one of the best ways to serve your fellow man is to protect them from the dangers of a crazy world and be willing to give your life. So, here I am about to embark on my third tour in Afghanistan. Though some guys from my unit believe we might get reassigned to Syria if the situation keeps worsening.

"So why the Marine Corps?"

"It's all in the uniform; the other three branches have pretty lame uniforms and if you're going to impress the ladies, you need some nice threads." Jack flashes that confident smile again.

"Ah, here comes Captain cool again"

"I thought it was Corporal cool?"

"Captain, Corporal, it's all the same shit isn't it?"

"No, but that's okay I guess, I won't be taking any orders from you." Jack adds a wink to that confident smile.

"Don't be too sure about that." She adds her own wink and a smile.

Their eyes meet in the stillness of the moment and it seems as if their eyes are growing together. Like a Whitesnake *looking* For *love...* they illuminate a unique feeling that seems to get to the core of their soul. That the eye isn't just a window to the soul… it is in itself a unique universe… an alternate or parallel universe… one that only a specific conscious being can see. Though people are only sub-consciously aware of this reality… we can feel it in our hearts. And why it is hard to stare someone in the eye for more than a few seconds. Because every individual needs their universe to be protected until trust has been fully established. And then they don't feel the need to hide who they are out of fear of judgement… they can see that person's soul for what it is … it is the connection to the consciousness of God. Even though Jack and Trinity barely know each other, there is no awkwardness as they see into the unique and beautiful universe found in the eyes. It seems as if their souls recognize that they are connected. Connected possibly from a past life… and quite possibly back to the moment of creation… when light and darkness separated from the Oneness of the Almighty.

A flash of light hits the window snapping them both out of the admiration for the beauty each has in their eyes. A soft rumble of thunder comes a few seconds later.

Trinity looks down at her plate and sees the food she prepared so perfectly to her liking. She closes her eyes and does the sign of the cross, but does it in an unusual way. She taps her forehead twice, then taps the center of her chest twice, then touches her left shoulder, and finally touches her right shoulder. Then she places her hands together and puts them underneath her lips, says a little prayer with the silent movement of her lips, and finishes with the sign of the cross again like she did before. Then she grabs her knife and fork to begin feasting on the blessed food.

Jack is really puzzled by this little ritual and wants to ask her about it, but he doesn't want to seem too judgmental towards her, so he also starts cutting up his pancakes and eating them with delight. He decides to throw out another question that he is curious about, as he tries to get to know her better. "So, did marijuana give you a rebirth into Christianity?"

"Yes and no… When I was adopted, I was raised Catholic and even went to a Catholic grade school. But for some reason, I never truly believed what I was being taught was actually real. The stories were too much like fairy tales and seemed no more real than Santa Claus. I just went through the motions for many years out of fear and guilt that religion tends to do to the young that don't understand how to comprehend such abstract thinking. I eventually got tired of the routine that didn't mean anything to me, so I walked away from my faith and basically became an agnostic. I couldn't go all the way to atheism and completely deny the existence of God, but agnosticism comes pretty close. I turned to science as the most effective way to interpret the meaning of this reality. And my job as a social science teacher only reinforced the idea that God didn't exist. Why would a God that supposedly loves us, let so much suffering in the world occur over the history of mankind? I was pretty content that our existence was pure chance and that we control all aspects of our lives. Then it happened... I had my direct encounter with God using marijuana and it made me believe that what I learned as a child is real, and that Jesus Christ is a savior for humanity. But it went beyond Christianity and I now started to see that all religions are right about their views on God. That they all basically preach the same idea, just in different languages, customs, and traditions. All major religions today talk about the Oneness of Almighty God. So yes, I am a Christian, but I could easily be a Muslim, or a Hindu, or any major religion that preaches the Oneness of God. I just focus on Christianity because it is the most familiar to me and the one I know the most about. But I don't follow any specific branch of Christianity and I have added my own unique rituals, that also include a little bit of Islam and a little bit of Hinduism."

Jack now seizes the opportunity and asks, "Was that what you did when you touched your head and chest twice when you made the Sign of the Cross... a unique ritual?"

"Yes, and very few people notice that. But when they do, I just tell them that I am balancing force. Most people just smile awkwardly at the Star Wars reference and let it go, but some want me to explain it more... like you."

"Ok, I'm game... how are you balancing the force that little ritual?"

"I am trying to uphold the Fifth Commandment of the Bible that says you should honor thy Father and thy Mother. "Can you guess how the ritual works?"

Jack pauses for a few seconds in thought, as he tries to figure out what would balance out the Sign of the Cross with the Fifth Commandment in her mind. "Would the second tap represent the Mother and Daughter?"

"Right again Jack! You are 3 for 3 now and have discovered the holy Trinity."

"Whoa... Wait a minute. So you are trying to tell me that the Fifth Commandment is not about honoring our earth parents, but it is telling us that God is both the spirit of a man and a woman and both need to be honored? Now I was raised Catholic too and I don't remember learning about that in Sunday school."

"Of course you wouldn't... We live in a male dominant world which not only includes political and economic aspects of society, it extends to many cultural aspects like religion. Look at how the Catholic Church won't allow for there to be female priests, even with a liberal Pope. Before the dawn of the monotheistic religions, people used to honor both male gods and female goddesses. But when God became just one entity, I guess men decided that God had to be a man. You could say women got sent to the darkness of hell where they are treated as second class citizens with little or no role to play with the divine."

"I can see your point, but your idea doesn't even fit with the Holy Trinity of Christianity which talks about the Holy Spirit and if you add a Mother and a Daughter to balance Father and Son, you will be making it four entities, not three.

"Well, if you look at the cross, there are four points to it. You could say each point refers to the 4 biological roles of the family (Father, Mother, Son, Daughter). I normally touch the head for the Father, then the heart for the Mother, followed by the Daughter on the left shoulder, and finish with the Son on the right shoulder. Every once in a while, I will switch it up and touch the forehead twice for the parents, then touch the heart twice for the Son and Daughter, and finish with the Holy Spirit by touching both shoulders. I just don't ever start with the son or daughter because I would be dishonoring the parents and violating the Fifth Commandment."

"So, you are saying the Holy Spirit is a woman and that there is a deception to hide this?"

"I'm saying that the Holy Spirit is the spirit or energy of God, and this spirit can come to us as a male or a female. But I believe the symbolic dove was used to hide women in the equation known as the Trinity. Probably to get rid of polytheistic Pagan beliefs that honored women."

"Ok, I can see some logic with the 4 points of the cross, but that still doesn't explain the Trinity well because there are only 3 points to a triangle, and if you add a daughter, you now have four.

"Maybe we should stop looking at the Trinity as a 2 dimensional triangle and start looking at it like the 3 dimensional world we live in."

Jack softly says, "A pyramid..." then there is a bright flash outside illuminating the window as Jack's eyes get wider with this discovery. A few seconds later you hear the rumble of thunder in the distance.

"Exactly, with each member of the family occupying a corner and working their way to the top of the pyramid... what you might call an ascending stairway to heaven, where they become One... they become Almighty God with the combined spirits of male and female, both parents and children. This is why I believe pyramids were built all over the world. It is a symbol of the quantum nature of God. As you go up to heaven to the Oneness of God, big things get smaller. God becomes invisible and is in its purest state... God is pure consciousness, powered by lightning."

She takes a quick sip of her coffee... "Now if you are looking for a 3 part Trinity... I do have one to offer, but they are concepts, not people. Want to hear them?"

Jack laughs a little in appreciation of her unique mind... "at this point, how could I refuse?"

"Ok!" Her eyes shine even more with light as the excitement she feels to reveal the secrets that are locked in her mind. "It starts with Trust at the top of the pyramid, followed by Faith in the right corner and Hope in the left. Trust is Oneness (no gender), Faith is Him, and Hope is Her. Now the only way to

Trust the Oneness of God is through Faith, but if you struggle and things get bad enough, Hope will come along to give you the strength to have Faith to Trust that God will provide for... or save you."

"Wow," Jack exclaims... "You definitely have an interesting theory, but good luck trying to convince over 2 billion Christians around the world about a theory you got while stoned."

"First of all, I know I can't convince people of anything. All I can do is share my experience and see what happens. Second, I actually didn't get that revelation while I was stoned, I told you earlier how I get information about God even when I am sober, it is just the most intense when I smoke pot." Another flash of light hits the window and a few seconds later, thunder rumbles a little bit louder than the last one. "I believe smoking marijuana opened something in my mind. I believe it opened up what is known as the 3rd eye; do you know what that is?"

"I've heard of it, it is supposed to open your mind up to the higher dimensions of the spiritual world."

"Yep, and biologically it is part of the brain called the pineal gland."

"So marijuana is needed to open up your pineal gland?"

"Well, marijuana might be one way... other drugs like DMT, LSD, ecstasy, and mushrooms could be other ways. And you can do it naturally, but that takes a lot of time and a disciplined lifestyle. You would probably have to do a lot of meditation, follow a strict diet, do yoga, and basically have a life like a Buddhist monk. Most people in the modern world won't take the time or effort to reach the state of awareness naturally. And one of the hardest things they would have to do would be to give up meat."

"Oh, like this bacon I have on my plate." Jack picks up a piece and takes an animal-like bite out of a strip. Then makes a funny face like he is a wild animal and growls at her."

Trinity laughs at this cute gesture and puts her hand by her mouth so she doesn't spit out any of her pancake. She can feel her heart melting like the butter on her pancakes as she connects with the fact he isn't afraid to be silly with her. He is exposing his soul to her without fear of rejection. It is almost a child-like state where we entertain people out of pure joy. It is the joy that many of us lose as we grow older because someone laughed at us instead of with us. So, we withdraw into hiding or we try to act cool to cover up what are now insecurities. She removes her hand from her mouth when she is done chewing, "I actually have a theory about that too, but I won't make you feel guilty right now for lowering your vibrational state. You can read it on my webpage if you want."

Another flash of light hits the window with the sound of thunder coming sooner and louder.

"Looks like that storm is getting closer, we might be stuck here for a while." Jack smiles knowing it gives him more time to talk to Trinity. His heart warms looking at the beauty found not only her eyes, but the light he can sense in her heart. He has never met someone so open about herself and wants to dig to dig deeper into the heart of her being.

Her eyebrows flash upward with a curious smile. "Or we could go for a ride in the heart of the storm and experience the fire in the rain up close... What do you say? Want to live a little?"

"Actually, I would love to live a lot... and riding in a thunderstorm might cause my early demise... yours too."

"I guess you don't have much faith that God has a plan for you, because if you did, you wouldn't be afraid to take a risk"

"Well, I believe taking on a third tour in Afghanistan shows that I am not afraid to take a risk."

"Touché Jack... but let me ask you something; do you have faith in God?"

"I already told you that I was raised Catholic."

"That doesn't mean you have faith, it just means you belong to an institution. Do you go to church?"

"I make it a couple times a year."

"Let me guess, Christmas and Easter?"

Jack gives a little bit of a guilty smile.

"Do you ever pray?"

"On occasion."

"Daily or just when you need something?"

The guilty smile returns on Jack's face.

"Looks like the cat has your tongue... how come?"

"I feel guilty... because I was taught to believe in God and it makes sense in my mind that there has to be something greater out there. I just don't see God in my daily life, so I focus on the things I need to do to make it in this world. It makes it hard for me to feel God like you do. I would like to feel God more, but I don't know how, so I guess I just put it out of my mind most of the time and just live my life."

A really bright flash hits the window followed by a loud thunder clap. Trinity jumps in her seat a little from the surprise.

Jack gives a sarcastic smile, "Do you still want to take a ride in the heart of the storm now that it seems to be arriving?"

"Ummm, yeah, maybe that wouldn't be the smartest thing to do right now... Sherry says it shouldn't be too long before it passes, maybe we can chase it a little after it passes by!" Her face lights up.

Jack sees the light in her eyes again and feels he is drawing even closer to her, because he subconsciously knows that the light comes from her heart. This causes the light in his heart to light up his eyes more and she feels the same towards him… they don't even know it, but this is the first steps of falling in love… when you connect with the love or light in someone else's heart.

"Did somebody call?" As Sherry approaches with a pot of coffee. "Would you guys like a refill?"

They both nod yes. As She refills their cups, another bright flash and thunder clap hits the window. "Looks like the storm arrived a little earlier than my phone said it was. You can never trust weather predictors."

Small raindrops start pelting the window and wiggle their way down the glass due to the force of gravity.

"Someday Sherry… we will be able to see into the future and accurately predict the weather."

"Ahhh, here we go, more of your theories about the power of the mind and how it relates to God." She looks over to Jack and talks to him like Trinity is not there. "She's a sweet girl, but might only have 50 cards in the deck." Then looks back at Trinity and gives a loving wink to her as she walks back to the kitchen.

Trinity barks back in a tender tone, "It's okay Sherry, you know I believe God is crazy too!"

"Do you really believe that?" Jack says with a bit of an offended tone.

"Of course." She gives a serious look back. "It helps me understand why the world is the way it is."

"How so?" Jack looks perplexed.

"First of all, look at any religion at a distance and examine their beliefs and practices. You will see that you have to go crazy to find God. Christianity has just as many crazy ideas as Scientology. Just because you have been around a lot longer and have over 2 billion followers doesn't mean you have lost the crazy. It just means people have been desensitized to it and it no longer really bothers anyone."

"Where do you see something crazy in how Christianity honors God?"

"The ritual of the Last Supper honors cannibalism and vampires. Just because they don't actually eat real human flesh and drink real human blood doesn't mean it isn't a crazy ritual. Now Christianity shouldn't be offended by what I am saying; if you step back and look at life and examine it closely… everything in life can be described as crazy… this is the true nature of God."

"Maybe, but suggesting God is crazy doesn't make much sense to accepted religious beliefs within modern society."

"It's all about perception… it's not crazy if you can find beauty in it. This is why people find the ritual of the Last Supper beautiful. They don't focus on the fact that it symbolizes eating a human body and drinking human blood, which is disgusting. It is about making the ultimate sacrifice (giving your life) to help your fellow human beings live (feeding them your energy)."

"Exactly." Jack acknowledges her comment.

"Now you could extend this way of thinking to other aspects of society like homosexuality. Many heterosexuals find homosexuality sinful and evil because they see some negative references written in holy books. But if they would just look at it as two human beings displaying love or bringing enjoyment to another person, then it is beautiful."

"But since there are negative references in their holy books, they think it goes against God's will."

"Don't forget these holy books were written by men in a much different time period and just because there were some homophobes back when these books were written, doesn't mean that God is a homophobe. God will evolve as humanity does, because God is the same as humanity. And as we become more accepting as time goes on… so will God."

"God evolves?"

"Yes… look at history for proof of that."

"I see your point about perspective and beauty"… Jack shakes his head in disbelief. "But to me, God doesn't evolve… God is everything that is good and beautiful and nothing crazy or evil."

"Do you truly believe that God is everything (in existence)?"

Jack pauses while he thinks, then says, "Yeah, most people that believe in God would agree to that."

"Well, if God is everything, then that would include a dark side where God is evil and does crazy things."

"Isn't that the job of the Devil, or Satan, or Lucifer… whatever you want to call him?"

"And who created that spirit?"

"Wasn't he a fallen angel that rebelled against God?"

"Are you sure that Lucifer is just a man?"

"That's what everyone believes?"

"Everyone once believed the earth was the center of the universe, so that doesn't mean they're right. Listen, we have a little bit of time until this thunderstorm passes. Do you want to hear my overall theory about God? I'll start from the beginning."

"Sure, how detailed is this theory? Should I get a pen and take some notes on this napkin?" Jack gets a smirk on his face.

She smiles at his little bit of sarcasm, loving the fact that he is not afraid to challenge her. "I'll give you the condensed version, and if you need more details, you can go to my web page. Ok, here it is… **God is clear.**" She then takes the last bite of her pancakes and chews while she lets Jack chew on what she just told him.

Jack sits there for a few seconds waiting for more, "sooo… that's it? God is clear."

She nods her head and finishes chewing with a smile, then takes a sip of her coffee.

"Are you going to elaborate a little or do you want me to think you are now down to 49 cards?"

She laughs. "You know how to flatter girls don't you? Ok, I'll give you a brief elaboration because we will be here for most of the night if I get too technical. God by all accounts is perfect; right?"

"Sure." Jack says with an obvious tone.

"Perfect would also mean pure, meaning God is free of all contaminants, which would also include color / light. So, God has to be clear, which means that God is invisible. And if this clear extends for eternity, we would call that a singularity (One dimension). So, in the beginning God was a singularity of almost pure darkness, or you might say invisible light. Now, the force (consciousness) of God is there, a single thought or vibration that came in the form *I AM* (if you use English), but God can't see itself because there was no light... God was blind and basically all alone in the darkness of Hell (with no real thoughts or experiences to define itself beyond a basic awareness). God was in almost pure darkness in the beginning and wanted to see, so God turned the lights on. So, the next step was God becoming a singularity of pure white light (using sound or vibrations to create thoughts). God created every possible thought extended to infinity, but that was too much light (too much information), and God was *blinded by the light.*"

Jack jumps in, "Like that song from the 70's that everyone thinks think says douche instead of deuce?"

"Yep, Bruce Springsteen I believe, then some other dude. So, God was blind again and realized it needed a balance of darkness and light to truly see. Then God, like the song says, *revved up like a deuce* and divided into two. God brought the two forces (dimensions of light and darkness) together in a form of sexual union. Now God allowed the darkness to almost completely engulf or compress the light, but not to the point where it becomes a singularity again. Once light exists, darkness can't snuff it out because light is eternal. Now, you have this really tiny ball of light that was all the light from the light dimension and you could call it the first star in existence. Scientifically, you could call it a super white dwarf. And if you take all the light from eternity and smash it down to a tiny ball, you are going to create an intense amount of heat and pressure and you have the conditions for a huge explosion. Then when the force of the darkness could no longer contain the pressure, the first star went supernova."

Jack's mouth drops a little with his face showing awe and says, "The Big Bang."

At the exact moment he says those 3 words; a sizzling crack of lightning flashes just outside the restaurant shaking the small tin can of a diner, causing Jack and Trinity to jump back in their seats.

"Oh my God, that scared the shit out of me!" Trinity exclaims.

Jacks looks down at his pants, "I'm just checking to see if I peed myself."

They both let out a big laugh, and the joy they are letting out of their hearts is once again noticed by each other in their eyes. They both feel the love (connection) that is growing between them.

Jack says in a skeptical voice, "What makes you believe this theory is real?"

Trinity responds in a confident voice, "God told me."

"Really? How, like a burning bush?"

She snickers, "Not directly, but through visions and clues."

"I understand how visions work, but God gave you clues... how, where?

"They're everywhere! You just have to be able to sense them."

Jack's tone changes to intrigue, "Give me an example."

"Well, you can obviously look at holy books from the past. The story of Genesis tells this. You can also look at scientific theory like the Big Bang. But the hardest clues to sense are the ones that are in the arts, mostly in movies, TV, and music. Like the song *Blinded by the Light*. When I first got my revelations back in September, I first thought that God started out as pure white light before God allowed darkness in to create space / time. But I changed my mind recently and went one step before almost pure white light to clear (almost pure darkness) when I heard the song *Dancer* by *Didrik Thulin (Kygo Remix)*. Do you want to listen to it?"

"Sure, why not."

Trinity reaches into her purse and pulls out her phone. She taps on the screen for about a minute, then hands the phone to Jack. "I got you the lyrics on my phone too." She then pulls out her wireless headphones, hands them to Jack, and he listens to the song while reading the lyrics.

(Listen to the song if you choose)

Jack takes the headphones out of his ears when the song is over. "Interesting song with a catchy tune, but that doesn't prove your theory is right just because one artist wrote some scientific terms like supernova and big bang in a song. Plus, I find it hard to believe this guy wrote this song to explain how all existence began."

"Well, have you ever heard artists talk about being inspired and the words just come to them?"

"Yeah, but I assume they mostly write about their lives."

"And if you believe in God; who ultimately influences our lives? Plus, we have all heard the saying that God works in mysterious ways, so maybe this is one way God works. Now there are many more examples I could show you, so it is not just one song from one artist. Part of my theory states that we are all God in microcosm. So, Almighty God continually works through all us to define this reality. So, when we write books, create music, movies, etc.; it is really God's imagination creating all of this stuff through us subconsciously. We are just too blind (unaware) to see it. And it takes our heart to make us aware of this reality. You obviously didn't feel the meaning of the song in your heart, you just processed the words and music in your brain."

"Well, what am I supposed to do? That's how my brain works when it processes information from my ears that hear sounds and my eyes that read words."

"What you need to do is connect your heart and brain better. This is what I believe the pineal gland does if you can open it. I believe the heart is a receiver of information too. Your heart receives information from higher dimensions or what people might call the spiritual world... the realm of God. The problem is it doesn't have neural connections to process the information into thoughts. It is information that is interpreted through feelings. I believe this is what most people feel is intuition, or maybe a hunch, gut feeling; whatever you want to call it. Now your brain gets a little confused because it is not processing information directly through the senses, so you brain does not know if it can trust the information. You have to learn to trust what your heart is telling you."

Jack still looks perplexed. "So opening your pineal gland is how you do it? Well, I don't have the time or energy to become a Buddhist Monk."

"I told you there is a short cut." She smiles with a look of anticipation of what he might say next.

"Drugs? I don't like that idea because drugs kill people. And I don't want to die unless it's in defense of my country or by natural causes."

Trinity nods her head a little. "I can respect that... and there are many dangerous drugs out there that can kill people. Alcohol and other drugs like heroin kill thousands each year from overdoses. And they are especially dangerous if you make a cocktail out of them. But there is one drug that has never killed a person from an overdose."

"Let me guess... pot."

"Precisely!"

"If it is not dangerous, then tell me why it is illegal."

"First of all, let me say that marijuana shouldn't be taken lightly. It's not a toy... and like with anything, if you abuse it, you can damage your body. Overindulgence is a bad thing and it doesn't matter what you are talking about... even purified water can harm you if you drink too much in a short period. Marijuana is a wonderful gift from God. It gives you an incredible high that intensifies all of your senses. This is why stoners get the munchies, because food tastes better. Music sounds better, comedy is funnier, video games are cooler, etc. But beyond the fun it provides, there is a huge list of benefits for society. There are many health benefits like controlling seizures. It has many industrial uses like using it to make paper. The problem is, it poses a threat to big profitable companies like the alcohol, tobacco, and pharmaceutical industries to name a few. So, these industries buy off our politicians through campaign contributions to keep it illegal. And they demonize it by saying it is some sort of gateway drug, which is a bunch of BS. You have to understand there is a lot of negative propaganda (fake news) out there about marijuana and if you don't do some research, you will believe it. Another issue you could run into if it were completely legal, is you could grow it yourself and then the government would lose out on a nice source of tax revenue. You don't have to process it much, so anyone could grow their own. Other drugs like alcohol need a lot more processing, so it's easier to just buy it in the store. It's mostly about the stupid way we do economics. If we didn't have such an inefficient, archaic way we control resources, pot would not be illegal."

"So, now you are saying economics is the problem and capitalism is inefficient? What are you a socialist… or a communist?"

"It's all connected and you have to look at the source of most of our problems in the world today… money. I actually believe all 3 major practices of economics today are inefficient and harmful. Why? Because they all use money, which is just an artificial means of control and it only works if there is scarcity. And scarcity only causes pain. But this is the reason why we can never produce anything efficiently and have abundance, because this would collapse the monetary economies we created. If we could put science to work and employ the best technology, we could create a society where all of our needs are met, without putting a price tag on anything."

"Wait a minute. You want an economy that has no money, where everything is free? That would never work."

"Sure it could if you are Living *things* that believe in the Mercedes *Marxist*. There is a man named Jacque Fresco, who I believe is 100 years old now, came up with an idea known as a Resource Based Economy and he has been promoting it since at least the 1970's. It uses the scientific method to create an efficient economy where we use the best technology to create abundance. And it can be done. If you want to see how, just go to his website called *The Venus Project*. We just have to **_choose_** as a global society to implement it."

"Good luck getting people to give up money, especially the rich."

"I know that's a tall order, but they would if they raise their vibrational consciousness to a more divine or higher level. And they would realize that a resource based economy would not take away their standard of living."

"And how might you raise your vibrational level? Pot again."

"Well, it takes more than just smoking pot, but that might get the ball rolling if they experience what I recently experienced from using marijuana. I just read a couple of books called the *Celestine Prophecy* and the *10th Insight* by an author named James Redfield. He gives some great ideas how a higher vibrational state of consciousness would also lead to a moneyless economy. Basically, he says that once people raise their energy levels or vibrational frequencies, the transition from a monetary economy to a moneyless economy would happen by people giving their services for free. Then relying on people donating to each other until the transition to a moneyless economy is complete. This is why I put my first book online for free after I had my rebirth. I believe my vibrational consciousness went up and understood this concept… even before I read those books. I felt the information needed to be shared with anyone, without any constraints."

"Well, has anyone donated to you yet?"

"No, because I needed to make people see that money wasn't why I shared it. So, I didn't provide a means to donate at first, like a Go Fund Me page. Now, my first book didn't have much of a story, nothing to draw them in emotionally, so most people that read it, didn't like it or they didn't get it. I was just some crazy blogger that very few people pay attention to and there are plenty of them out there. Plus, I hadn't read the *Celestine Prophecy* yet, so I didn't understand how we might transition to a moneyless economy. But now that I do, I want to be an example of how to transition from a monetary economy to a resource based (moneyless) economy."

"How much of a donation are you going to ask for?"

"The same amount that street performers ask for… I will give them a hat (like a Go Fund Me page) and they can donate however much they want to. Give them the choice, which is how it should be. It's basically how I earn money on stage at the club. Most people give a dollar, some give fives or tens, but your friend George gave me a $20 after my dance on stage tonight."

"So, you want the world to turn into a bunch of street performers? Where they provide a service or labor and ask for donations or tips?"

"Yes! They perform because they love it and want to share it with the world or they just want to help. I recently talked to this starving musician named Zach Pietrini who gave a free concert at a small church and asked for tips at the end. I can tell you more about him later, but he proves that this is our human nature… if we have knowledge or a talent, we don't want to keep it to ourselves… we want to share it. Now, because we do currently live in a world defined by an artificial control mechanism (money), this is why street performers put out the hat. But if all of their needs were met (food, clothing, shelter, energy, health care), they would do it for free because they still want to perform. It's like when you see kids performing in whatever they love… they don't get paid. But as we get older, we are brainwashed into believing that we won't be motivated to perform or help if we don't get paid for it. That if we didn't have money to motivate us, we would sit around and watch TV all day long getting fat. Kids prove that way of thinking wrong every day. We need to break from that way of thinking because it destroys our true human nature. Our true human nature is to share and to give, not to hoard and be selfish."

"If this method you are talking about is so great; why didn't your web page book take off?

Trinity gets a look of concern on her face. "Well, I didn't realize how hard it is to get your ideas noticed or go viral using a blog page; so currently, I am going to self-publish my new book and hope it takes off using a more traditional method. Now, this goes against what I am proposing people do because I will obviously earn income from it, but I'm not insane and you know the definition of insanity... right?"

Jack laughs a little, "Yep, it's where you keep trying the same thing expecting different results."

"Exactly, and I realize that maybe the best way to get my messages out there is to do it in small steps and use methods that the majority of people accept. I need to become an established author like Dan Brown, who is pure genius in my mind. Now if Dan would have just created a blog and talked about his theory about the DaVinci Code... nobody would have taken him seriously. They probably would've said he stole everything from those guys that wrote the book *Holy Blood, Holy Grail,* and said he is just plain crazy. So, he created a creative story that drew people in and captivated their attention and became one of the most famous authors in the world. This is what I believe God has done with creating holy books from around the world. Reveal things slowly using incredible creative stories. If you reveal things too quickly and don't bring them in emotionally, people will reject it and think you are crazy. I'm really starting to understand this vague concept... what we like to call evolution. And hopefully we can evolve to a world where the necessities of life are provided for... free of charge."

Jack still looks perplexed. "Well, not everything is this world is a service; some things take hard labor and who is going to do that stuff for free?"

"Automation will eventually be able to do all the hard labor, but until we become fully automated, people would need to volunteer to help. You can see this effort when disasters happen (ie. tornadoes, earthquakes, 9-11, etc.) and people don't ask to get paid. It's just sad that most people won't volunteer to help unless it's some kind of tragedy. This could change if people achieve a higher state of awareness."

"Ok, that is a noble idea and may be a possibility down the road... but getting back to the subject of marijuana... another problem I run into about using pot is I have heard it lowers your IQ."

"Well, I am not a brain researcher, so I can't comment on that. But through personal experience, I can say it does hurt your memory some, but I don't believe it hurts your overall IQ. I think that is a bunch of BS and just a stereotype that is portrayed in movies and TV. Some of the smartest people I know smoke pot. Plus, you have the likes of really smart famous people who support and use marijuana like the late Carl Sagan, author Stephen King, and even Bill Maher, to name a few."

"Bill Maher, the comedian? You think he's smart. He's just a liberal blowhard if you ask me."

"Well, have you ever watched his show... Real Time?"

"Nope."

"Well, try it sometime when you get back from this latest tour of duty."

Jack gives her a smile of appreciation. "I'm glad you said when." He feels even more drawn to her inner beauty that always seems to look at the bright side.

Trinity smiles back, "I'm a believer in being positive." She pauses a little wishing that this encounter that is developing into love has a positive ending. She reminds herself to have faith in God's plan and if her and Jack are to be together. She then continues, "now, you might not agree with Bill's views on certain issues, but the man is wicked smart. I watch his show religiously even though I don't agree with him about God anymore. He's an atheist. But he is by far one of the best debaters I have ever seen."

"Do you think you think you could convince him to believe in God?"

"Well, the one thing I have learned through this experience, is you can't tell people what to believe. You have to get them to think so they will question their own beliefs. Then they will change on their own if the seed you plant in their mind grows and blossoms. It's kind of like the premise of the movie *Inception*, if you have seen it."

"Yeah, that was a great movie that really made you think about the nature of reality."

"Now, I believe I could have a chance at convincing Bill that God exists because I believe I understand reality better than I ever have and can explain things on a much higher level. When my new book takes off, Bill might decide to have me on his show because he is a big-time advocate for the legalization of marijuana and then I could have a little debate with him about the existence of God. Or I could smoke with him after the show and teach him how I did it, which might help him meet God personally, because I was in the same boat he was for a long time... a nonbeliever."

"There is a method on how to meet God using marijuana?"

"Maybe. Now I wasn't ever a big user of pot, but I have done it off and on since I was 18 and never felt any connection to God. It just happened to be a few months ago that I experienced a connection that could only be described as divine. It was way beyond anything that I ever experienced in the past and it changed me profoundly. Now I retraced what happened so there might be a method to it, but I don't know because I haven't tried it with anyone else." She pauses and then says with a hesitant voice, "Would you like to be my guinea pig?" As she gives a smile of anticipation that he will say yes.

Jack leans back in the seat with a look of indecision. "You definitely have my curiosity, but I can't; I leave for the Middle East soon and could be drug tested before I go."

"Well, you say you have never smoked before and I've heard if you're not a regular user, there won't be much in your system. Then if you drink a bunch of water in the morning plus some coffee and go to the bathroom a few times, it will flush most of it out and you will pass the test."

"Is that guaranteed or just a guess; because I don't want to pop a hot pee test and be discharged… that will follow me the rest of my life."

"Nothing is guaranteed Jack except death and taxes, at least in this point in time." She now leans back a little and gives him a look that says I dare you. "The question is… do you want to take a risk? You are a bit like Joel in the movie Risky Business right now. You have an opportunity to have a life altering experience… but you have to be able to say what the fuck, in order to make it happen."

"What if I do and I get caught, it could possibly ruin my life?"

"Well, you have to look at the bright side then. Maybe it will save your life. You obviously are entering a very dangerous part of the world and you might not come back. Have you ever heard of people that have a very strong feeling about doing something, like not getting on an airplane, then the plane crashes and they are so happy that they followed their gut and are still alive… So, what is your gut telling you to do?"

"Honestly, my gut is telling me to give it a try. But my brain is telling me not to because I will get caught."

"This is where I have learned to trust God and follow my gut… really my heart… because this is where I believe God is mostly found. Do you have faith that there is a greater plan for you? Maybe one greater than being a soldier? This is why I ultimately quit my teaching job. I decided to trust God that my destiny is greater than the career I established and maybe leaving a job where I had a lot of security was the risk I needed to take. I decided to follow the signs that would lead me to a greater destiny. This is what I also realized when I read the *Celestine Prophecy* and the *10th Insight*. It made me believe that I was following a greater path, one that might really make a difference in this world. You just have to get past the fear first."

"That is a fictional novel; how can you trust that?"

"It is fictional, but that doesn't mean the message behind it isn't real. You could argue that a lot of the Bible is fictional too, but that doesn't stop millions, possibly billions of people from following those ideas."

You can see by the look on Jack's face that his defensive wall is starting to crumble. "So, if I do this and get caught, it was part of God's plan for me?"

"That's how I look at everything now and let me tell you, it is completely liberating! To know that I don't have to control my destiny… give it up to a higher power… that is true faith… and it will bring you true freedom…I have never been happier in my life."

"So, you don't believe being an exotic dancer is your destiny?" He smiles hoping she doesn't take it in a bad way.

Trinity laughs, "God no! It's just a way to bring in some income while I get my true destiny going."

"And what is that? To be a writer?"

"Not just a writer… I want to start a global movement."

"What kind of a global movement?"

Trinity seems to miss the question as she looks out the window, "Hey! The storm has passed us and is heading out to the ocean, why don't we chase the fire in the rain now? It will give you a chance to contemplate if you want to knock of heaven's door later with me and see the edge of the Kingdom. Plus, we are the only ones left in the diner and I'm sure Sherry and the cook want have some privacy." She raises her eyebrows up and down a couple of times with a sexy smile.

Jack gives a little chuckle.

Trinity yells over to Sherry who is behind the counter busy looking at her phone. "Hey Sher, we're ready to pay the bill and we can tell you and Sam want some alone time!"

Sherry looks up and scoffs, "like he would ever have a chance at that… Hell would have to freeze over!"

You can see Sam in the rectangular cutout in the wall just shaking his head back and forth in mockery as he cleans up the grill.

Sherry then walks over and places the bill on the table, "You guys have a great night." She then looks at Jack. "Hey handsome, make sure you get this sweet girl home safely on that motorcycle of yours… she likes to convince people to take chances and motorcycles aren't the best on wet roads."

Jack smiles and nods his head, "You bet." Then Sherry walks away.

Jack says to Trinity, "I got this," pulls out his wallet and leaves the money for the bill adding a nice tip on the table. Then smiles at Trinity and says "Sherry deserves her hat to be filled a little."

Trinity gives a smile back in appreciation for him acknowledging her idea.

They walk outside and feel the rain as a light drizzle now, but can see the flashes of lightning now heading towards the deep darkness of the ocean sky.

Trinity gazes upward, "Let's go… watching a thunderstorm head out to sea is really cool."

"How far do you live from here?" Jack asks.

"The beach house I rent is about 10 minutes east of here. You be Mav and I'll be Goose… just don't let what happened to Goose in the movie, happen to me."

"I have the Top Gun soundtrack on my playlist. I'll play *Danger Zone* while I ride to remind myself not to fly by the seat of my pants."

"Would you like to listen to another song that I believe has secret meaning about the story of God in the beginning? You can listen to it while we chase the storm towards my beach house."

"Ok, I enjoy riding with music."

"It's called *Fire in the Rain*, by *Mans Zelmerlow*."

"Wow that's weird, I listened to a song of his in the lobby at the club while I was waiting for you. I think it is called *Wrong Decision*. It was given to me by my music provider."

"Yep, I have that on my playlist... it's a good tune. And I'm thinking that might be a sign that you and I are connecting or are connected on a deeper level. Now, to me... this song talks about how God who is now split into two (light / male) and (darkness / female) and how they fell in love. And in order to make their love real (and not just a dream), they had to create this universe (and all life in it). But they had to take a dangerous road and separate (creating a space), with him going to heaven and her going hell (and in a way, losing her life by separating from the light). But she can now also give life (to humanity). But their love endures when they can both see each other (in the evening when darkness and light meet up), they remember the love they made to create the lightning (fire) that creates all life (consciousness). It was worth it to them, because it allows the consciousness they created on earth to find love. Ultimately, God (both forces) lives vicariously through us on earth, where everything is real."

Trinity takes out her wireless headphones again and hands them to Jack. "Now when you listen, don't just use your brain... see if you can feel the emotions in your heart by remembering the story I just told you."

Jack smiles, "Ok, I'll try to be like Luke attempting to destroy the Death Star, when Obi Wan tells him to let go and trust his feelings."

Trinity smiles back, "Now that's the spirit... see, you are starting to find clues yourself from movies."

Jack puts the headphones in his ears and they hop on his motorcycle for her beach house. Trinity hits the play button.

As they ride off towards her beach house, the night sky keeps lighting up with flashes that look like Fire *in the* Rain.

When that song ends, the next song on Trinity's playlist starts as they keep riding. It is another song by *Mans Zelmerlow – Happyland*.

(listen to the songs if you choose)

CH 3 – THE CHOICE...
OF ENLIGHTENMENT

Jack and Trinity pull up to her beach house right about when the song Happyland ends. They get off his Ducati and Jack pulls out the headphones in his ears and hands them back to Trinity. He looks around and sees a series of luxurious beach houses that are 3 stories tall with the garage on the bottom floor towards the road. Flashes of lightning still illuminate the sky even though the storm is well out to sea by now.

Trinity puts the headphones back in her purse, "So what do you think?"

Jack is looking at the grandeur of the beach house she directed him to. "This is quite a beach house!"

"Not the house silly," as she smacks him in the arm in a playful flirtation. "What did you think of the song that was playing in your ears as we were chasing the thunderstorm out to sea?"

"Yeah, I liked the song. The guy has a really good voice. And I could kind of hear what you saying, but I can't say it touched me in any special way. I would guess he was singing about someone special to him. His spouse or lover maybe?"

"That's probably true, but I told you that God works through us subconsciously and sends little messages about the nature of reality. Like I said before, my divine encounter helps me see these hidden messages now. You just need to get your heart and brain tuned to the same frequency and you'll start to see things more clearly. Let's walk around to the beach so we can see the thunderstorm disappear into the darkness."

"I'm game to watch the light show disappear," says Jack.

They walk down the sidewalk that leads to the beach side of the house where you can now hear the peaceful sound of the ocean waves crashing into the shoreline. Off in the distance you can see the thunderstorm sending traces of light across the sky, but the sound of thunder has ceased. It almost looks as if heaven is dimming the lights so darkness could come alive.

When they get to the beach, Jack reflects back on the motorcycle ride. "There was another song that played after, I believe it was called Happyland."

"That's one of my favorites! Did you hear the meaning behind the song?"

"Well, he said happy a lot. So, I'm guessing he is referring to heaven?"

"Yes, but what about heaven?"

"It sounded like it was damaged, there was a hole in the soul and a scar in the heart of it. And that we fucked it up... well."

"Yep... my interpretation tells me this is where Almighty God split into the spirits of man (light) and woman (darkness) and then were separated to create the physical universe (space / hole). This damaged the love (connection) between them. You could also look at it scientifically with a possible black hole that was created in the center of the universe when the first star went supernova. Now the part where he's says we fucked up is interesting because I believe he is sending a hidden message there. If you look at the written lyrics, Mans is singing wel...come to Happyland. But he pauses in the middle of the word so it sounds like he is saying that we fucked up well. And I may be wrong about this, but I have listened to it many times and it really sounds like he is saying that we fucked up well... going to Happyland. He also talks about how we became a one-man band before that line. So, my interpretation is that when God separated into two forces, this allowed for human consciousness to eventually separate from the Oneness of God; it forced us out of paradise. Now to get a little taste of heaven on earth, we can have some good sex, which is how we create life and experience what it is really like to be God. See, all of us are a little tiny microscopic part of the ultimate consciousness of Almighty God, so you could say that we are all God. We have just forgotten this so it causes us pain and we go to church to numb it."

When they get to where the waves are crashing up on shore, Trinity takes off her shoes, pulls up her sweat pants a little, and walks into the ocean. "Oh my God the water is freezing! Want to go for a swim?" She says in a joking tone.

"Yeah...ummm... I'll pass. It is definitely pleasant tonight, but it is still February." Jack pauses and looks up into the clearing sky to see the stars and moon light up the darkness. "So, you believe I am God?"

"Yep, along with the 7.5 billion other people on the planet, plus all other consciousness, like animals, insects, plants, bacteria, etc. Humans are just the most conscious of reality and obviously have the ability to shape the world how we want to... like no other living being can."

"I don't feel like a God."

"You know I really love the ocean, because it really makes me understand God so much easier. Almighty God is the ocean... and if I were to go inside and get a glass, I could come out and dip it into the ocean. The glass would fill up with ocean water. It is still the same water, but now it is separate from the Oneness of the ocean. So, all you need to think is that our bodies are made of glass and the conscious light that is inside each one of us, is the same light from the infinite ocean of consciousness from the Almighty."

Jack smiles, then squats down to where the waves are washing water up to the tips of his boots. He reaches down and touches the ocean water with his right hand. "Sometimes I wonder why I am here, why we are all here; there doesn't seem like there is much of a purpose, especially when you see so much suffering in the world." Jack then stands back up.

"It's simple," Trinity walks out of the water and stands really close to Jack, looking up into his eyes. "God needs us." She takes both of his hands into hers. "So God can know that its real through actual experience... like falling in love."

Jack looks into her eyes deeply and knows what he is starting to feel in his heart. His heart starts singing in his mind... everything will be alright... if I could Kiss *you* Tonight... as he bends his head down to hers slowly and gives her a tender kiss. Though the kiss warms his heart, he starts to feel a pain develop there, as he realizes the reality of the situation. He is leaving tomorrow for quite a long time with a strong possibility that he will never see her again. He slowly pulls back his kiss and looks out towards the ocean. "So why would God bring me to you tonight knowing that I would start feeling this way... knowing I was leaving for Afghanistan soon... it seems cruel."

Trinity gently turns his head back with her left hand on his cheek and with says with a loving tone, "because pain and suffering are part of making this universe feel real. Without it, we might only believe it is a dream. And when you finally go to Heaven to be with God, you will know that is real too because you will have experienced the pain and suffering of Hell. You need to go through Hell first in order to know Heaven is real." She then takes her hand off his cheek and puts it on the back of his neck, pulls him towards her and gives him a long and tender kiss in return. When she finally pulls back her kiss, she looks out at into the ocean with the thunderstorm barely flickering in the distance. "This is where my faith in God's plan helps me deal with a moment like this. If God's plan for me is to be with you, then you will return safely to me."

"I wish I could trust God like you do."

"Well, I could help you try to get in touch with God the way I did. Did you decide if you want to take the risk we talked about earlier?"

Jack takes one last quick glance out at the ocean and says with a hint of hope, "God's plan huh?" Then he turns back and gives her a loving closed lip smile and simply nods his head slightly up and down.

Trinity grabs his right hand with her left and they walk back to the beach house where she unlocks the door to the bottom level entrance. When the door opens, you hear the rumble of 8 feet coming down the stairs from the upper level. Two Border Collies run up to Trinity as she gives them some kisses on the top of their heads. They also check out Jack and sniff him to make sure he is safe to let in the house. One Border Collie is a larger with brownish red color intermixed with white. The other is smaller in size with black and white colors.

"So who are these guys?" Jack bends over to pet the larger Border Collie and the dog jumps up and licks his chin.

"That's Phoenix and the puppy is Kramer."

"Is that their real names?" Jack says with a touch of sarcasm and then starts to pet Kramer.

Trinity laughs, "Well the older one who seems to really like your chin, just turned 3 and was first named Hawk from the shelter. But I decided to change it to Phoenix because that is the greatest bird of existence and why settle for less of a bird. Then I got a puppy when I moved here so Phoenix would have company when I am working at the club. I named him Cosmo Kramer because I am a big fan of Seinfeld and the mysteries of the cosmos. But on the show, he is simply known as Kramer, so I just go with that."

Trinity quickly lets the dogs out to do their business after being locked up for quite a few hours. Jack starts to look around the 1st floor of the beach house and notices how nice it is. There is a bar and pool table, along with a huge rectangular couch surrounding a very large flat screen mounted to the wall. There are also two guest bedrooms, a bathroom, and a workout area with a fancy workout machine. When Trinity comes back in with the dogs, they head upstairs on the side of the house to the main level where there is one big open area with very high ceilings. He notices the large open space that is only separated by 2 large pillars and a small wall that provide support to the building. Large windows encompass the outside walls to let in light from all directions. As he does a 360, he takes notice of the beautiful kitchen in the middle, a dining area that is on the side of the house that faces the road, and a huge family room with a large screen TV over the fireplace. Surrounding the fireplace are large windows that unveil a beautiful deck. But even more beautiful, beyond the deck, is the majesty of the ocean that now shimmers from the light of the moon. The thunderstorm that was lighting up the sky with fire in the rain has now disappeared into oblivion. A peaceful feeling settles over Jack as he examines his surroundings. Trinity is playing with the dogs in the kitchen and giving them some treats, but for some reason, he can't really hear her and it feels as if time is slowing down. Jack starts to truly enjoy the silence and a single thought enters his mind in the form of a question... am I...in heaven...? This thought in the silence starts to feel like it could last an eternity...

Trinity unknowingly breaks the silence with a question of her own. "So, what do you think of my bachelorette pad?"

"It's incredible." Jack walks into the kitchen. "What does the rent run for something like this?... if you don't mind me asking?"

"Honestly, I couldn't afford this place if it wasn't for my best friend from the club. You actually met her tonight, but were not formally introduced. She could tell you wanted to talk to me at the table, so she left without a word. Her real name is Sarah, but her nickname is Kitten because she loves cats and can be shy and mysterious like them. She has a regular customer who is a wealthy hedge fund manager from New York. He owns this place and comes down a few times throughout the year. He rents it out to vacation goers while he mostly stays in the big city making millions magically appear through the investment game of our wonderful economy." Trinity says that with some sarcasm. "He's divorced and in his early 60's, but you wouldn't guess that because he takes wonderful care of himself. He truly adores her and is the main reason why she is having problems with her boyfriend. When I talked to her about my job situation, she convinced him to rent this place to me for a fraction of what he could get through the vacation market. This is the down time of the year so he agreed to it and is charging me $1000 / month, but I have to be out by the end of March when the weather really starts getting nice. This was just to help me establish myself here while I save a little money and finish my book. When her boyfriend found out about this, he speculated that she went beyond the lap dances at the club and he became suspicious. He believes guys only do nice things for girls to get that one thing and now has a hard time trusting her."

"Well, if I am being honest, I would feel the same way... most people only do things to get something in return." Jack pauses for a couple of seconds. "Do you think she slept with him to get you the deal?"

"She told me that she didn't and I have never known her to lie to me, but everyone has their dark side that they want to hide from others." Trinity then pauses for a couple of seconds. "What is something from your dark side Jack?"

Jack looks down and wonders if he should reveal something that might make her not feel good about him anymore. But for some reason, he feels like she will not judge him. He starts to sense that this is how you get someone to truly trust you. Tell them your darkest secrets... lay them on the table... and know that if they accept you for who you are and not run away... you will never have to deceive them. So, he takes a little bit of a deep breath and says in a regretful tone, "I enjoy killing people."

Trinity doesn't show any sign of shock or disappointment on her face. In fact, her eyes start to swell up with water as she feels deep compassion for Jack. She gives him a hug with her head turned sideways on his chest trying to hear the beating of his heart and so he can't see a couple of tears run from her eyes down her face. "Is that why you keep going back to the Middle East?... It gives you a license to kill?"

Jacks eyes now start to swell with water. "Before I met you tonight, while I was outside the club waiting for Dale and George to arrive; I was having a cigarette and I fantasized about going back to Afghanistan and taking out some bad guys. It's like when you watch a movie and the hero is there standing next to the bad guy who has done some truly terrible things and has the gun pointed at the bad dude's head. The hero has a choice... do you kill him and rid the world of this evil, or do you turn him over to the authorities? Well, I get a rush out of not turning the bad guy over to the authorities. The problem is... when you are in a war, not all the people killed are bad guys. Some are innocent children. This really bothered me when I first went over there, but now I have grown numb to this. Especially as I watched many of my brothers die from roadside bombs, suicide bombers, and sniper fire. Now I just see them as future terrorists that will try to harm my brothers and fellow Americans. It's almost to the point where I want to wipe them all out so I can feel assured that I can go home and sleep... peacefully. But I am starting to now wonder if I am still a *Man... Or...* am I turning into *A Monster?*" A tear runs out of his right eye and down his cheek. He then lays that cheek on the side of her head which is facing the opposite direction... they embrace in silence with their eyes closed. *(listen to a song that reminds you of a time when you were troubled by thoughts of being a monster. Close your eyes and listen to the words – try to feel what Jack is going through – don't continue reading until the song is over)*

Jack opens his eyes and notices two copper Moscow Mule mugs sitting on the counter. One is upside down and resting on top of the other and the handles are lined up, but pointing away from the edge of the counter. They step away from their embrace and wipe the tears off their faces. Jack tries to lighten the mood and change the subject. He points at the two mugs and says, "are you creating a potion in there or is it some sort of New Year's decoration that you haven't taken down yet?" A small smile emerges from what was a sad face just a moment ago.

Trinity erases her sad face and smiles back, then says, "You're close... I'm creating my own holy water so I can turn it into my version of the Blood of Faith."

"Another ritual? Does it go with your Sign of the Cross and the prayer where you combine Christianity, Islam, and Hinduism?"

"Yes, I blend quite a few different religions and rituals together in my own unique way."

Jack has a look of concern. "Aren't you afraid that you will be offending these religions and their followers by doing this? You are going to get a lot of backlash if you write about these things and promote the idea of creating a new religion that combines different faiths and rituals."

"I guess you could say I am creating a new religion, but understand something, I only want **one** follower of this new religion...Me. Now, if enough people want to know my techniques, I will share them, but I truly want people to find their own way to God. This is a personal journey; so why should any religion be offended by what I do to get closer to God? I am doing these rituals in the privacy of my own home. Now if I went to one of their holy buildings and started to do my rituals or preach to them that their rituals are wrong and my way is the proper way to get to God... now I can see them getting offended."

"Isn't your book going to be about how you found God and tell others how to do it?"

"I just want to show people that you can release God that is locked up inside you and that you don't have to rely on others to tell you what to believe and how to act. And this extends to all aspects of life. Too many people look to others to tell them what to do, whether its politics, economics, or cultural aspects like religion. Maybe we do that so we can blame others when we fail and not take a good look in the mirror and realize that maybe we are the problem. And realize, when you give others control over your thoughts and actions, you are not free, even if you fly a big red, white, and blue flag from a giant pole in front of your house."

"But won't there be complete chaos if people do whatever they want and don't have leaders to tell them what to do?"

"Not if they understand the concept of the Oneness of God. The ultimate connection of everything in the known universe and beyond to the scope of everything in existence. And that your thoughts and actions impact others in ways that you cannot fathom. Its known as the butterfly effect. An effect that can set forth a chain reaction that will have impacts that could actually effect the entire world. I wrote about that concept in my online book. Once people truly understand this idea, they will start treating each other like many religions promote around the world – treat others how you want to be treated. This is what love really is… feeling a connection to something else besides yourself and treating it like it is you. Because in true reality, this is what God really is… connection… Oneness."

"Don't you believe that way of thinking will destroy religion as we know it, possibly even society?"

"Current economics and government? Possibly, but I am not a threat to religious institutions or cultural uniqueness. In fact, if major religions wouldn't try to force their beliefs on people through fear and guilt or fight people finding their own way to God, their numbers would actually grow and church attendance would rise dramatically. Before I found my own way to God, I actually walked away from religion and I vowed that I would never walk inside a church again unless it was for a funeral or wedding. But when I found God on my own, I wanted to go to church and look forward to it now because I see the importance of being with a community of believers. And because God is so vast and complex (because God is infinite), I love hearing other perspectives about God. And when I go, I really listen to what is going on because I find meaning in it now. I have even visited a variety of different religions and gone to different churches within Christianity because I love seeing their perspectives on the Almighty. This is why I believe all religions that promote the Oneness of God are correct. Now, I am respectful and do not participate in their specific rituals (unless invited), because I am not a true member of their institution."

"But can't only one belief about God be right? You can't have everybody being right about God."

"Well, that is like saying that there can only be one way to be entertained. Maybe we should just have one sport to play then, one genre of music to listen to, etc. I wrote an analogy in my online book that talks about how we get food. We need food to survive; but is there only one grocery store that we can get food from? You walk into any grocery store and it doesn't matter what the name is on the outside, the food products are basically all the same. And is there just one road that leads to that store? No! But somehow, most people believe there is only one institution or one way to get to God and some are even willing to kill complete strangers over it. That is insanity if you ask me. And even science is a way to find God… it is just going to take them a lot longer to figure that out. But science will eventually start to prove the existence of God. The day that science, religion, and every culture on earth come together and understand that they all play a role in defining existence, that will be the moment we take our next step in evolution.

"Do you want people to all think the same? We would become like robots."

"Understanding Oneness is not thinking the same and giving up your cultural or individual differences. It's about accepting those differences because we all come from the same source and not trying to force them into your way of thinking. Right now there are too many people that want us to be just one religion, or one race, or one way to get married, and it just causes hatred and suffering. Ultimately it is fear that drives this. The books I told you about earlier, the *Celestine Prophecy* and *10th Insight* explain this very well. And once we are able to overcome the fear, we stop trying to gain each other's energy by controlling them. It is a brilliant way to look at what drives people to do awful things. Heck, even Yoda talked about how fear is a path to the dark side."

"Isn't that the Devil's job?" Jack takes a deep look into Trinity's eyes, "You know… you never really answered my question when we were back at the pancake house."

"Well, I decided to start at the beginning with an overall theory and then we obviously went off on different tangents and I forgot to go back to it."

"Let's go back to that then; who do you believe Satan is?"

"Dark Energy or evil thoughts that come from the Oneness of Almighty God."

"God has evil thoughts?"

"Yes, and why I believe part of God is crazy too. God is bipolar."

"God is bipolar?" Jack expresses a tone of shock.

"Yes, God had to become bipolar (2 opposite entities) in order to create the physical universe where thoughts can manifest themselves into physical reality. It's all about energy and it comes in good forms, or high vibrations of light… and bad forms, or low vibrations of darkness. Without low vibrational darkness, there would be too much high vibrational light and God would be blinded by the light.

"So you believe all darkness is evil?"

"No, in order for there to be balance, darkness had to become the dominant energy / matter in the universe. Most of the energy had to turn invisible or become dark so God could see clearly. I believe evil is part of dark energy and not some red dude with horns and a tail. Human consciousness likes to define things and make them familiar. We create understanding by giving our brains something to imagine that has definition. So, there is no old dude with a white beard in the clouds that is a good and loving God either. In fact, all the images and names we have given God over the years are just that, a way to define the undefinable *(think: Almighty God)*. And we went from many images and names (polytheism) to a more evolved idea (monotheism) and we have been narrowing down God to its true nature over time, or what science calls evolution. One that is basically nameless and formless, that encompasses every possible idea. I like to use the term Oneness, but I believe the Bible even gives a better name for God... *I AM*."

"*I AM*? The name God told Moses to tell the Israelites if they ask who sent you?"

"It's brilliant! Think about it... you can put anything behind it. *I AM* a man, *I AM* a woman, *I AM* a dog, *I AM* a Muslim, *I AM* gay, *I AM* transgender, *I AM* an atheist, *I AM* hate, *I AM* love, *I AM* bipolar, *I AM* good, *I AM* evil, *I AM* etc. You can take it out to infinity and now you have what God really is... One thought (starting with *I AM*) equals Infinite thoughts. It's actually a very simple math equation." She pulls a pen out of her little purse and writes on a small sheet of paper...

$$I\,AM = One = Infinity = Almighty\ God$$

Jack looks at the paper and gives a facial expression that says he is impressed by her creativity, but then turns to an expression of skepticism... "Once again, if you say this to people, many are going to backlash against you because they believe God is all good and is separate from evil."

"God is all good thoughts too, but realize, if we do anything on earth, good or bad, God is the one that thought it up first and put it into the cosmos for us to tap into. Now God gave us the choice or free will to let it pass or to embrace it and manifest it in the real world. And realize that good and bad is a matter of perspective too."

"What do you mean put it in the cosmos?"

"Have you ever heard of the multiverse, or parallel universes?"

"Aren't they alternate universes where other possibilities of reality happen?"

"Basically... and God gave us the ability to pull any ideas from other universes and manifest them into this universe by the effort we put into creating them. But it all starts with an idea that Almighty God already put into the multiverse, or what I like to call, the dream world. You want to build a skyscraper in a big city like the President used to do? You...(let's call you Micro-God), have to imagine what it will look like or in reality, pull in what Almighty God imagined first and stored in the multiverse. Then you need to draw it up (in a mathematical way) so others will understand Micro-God's idea. Then you need raw materials and labor to build it and wallah... it becomes real. This is how dreams from the multiverse become reality in this universe... its actually really simple."

"I guess it is." Jack gives a smile and says, "Do you have any beer? I'm starting to Lose *my* Mind and imagining I am getting a little thirsty and need a physical manifestation of a tasty liquid."

Trinity laughs at his witty sense of humor and replies, "I don't have any alcohol because I don't drink... it lowers my vibration. But I could manifest a soft drink for you? I also imagined (when I was at the store) that I have orange juice, and there is always good ole filtered water that manifests itself from the fridge."

Jack smirks at her witty reply, shakes his head and says, "Alcohol and meat?... I guess I'm doomed to stay at a low vibrational state then. I'll just take some water, and we better get going with this little experiment of yours because it is starting to get late and I need to sober up before I ride back to my parent's house. I gotta get up early so I can get back to Quantico by noon and get ready for my departure back to hell."

"Yes Sir, Captain, Corporal Cool! As she straightens up and gives him a military salute. "And if you are not sober enough to ride home to your parent's house, you can always crash here, I have 5 bedrooms, well... 4 guest bedrooms you can choose from." She gets a glass out of the cabinet and fills it from the dispenser on the fridge door and hands it to him.

"Thanks", and as he drinks down the water, he wonders if she might want him to stay the night for other reasons. He feels they are connecting on a much deeper level and senses the energy that is flowing between them. And with him leaving tomorrow, maybe this will be their only opportunity to share the ultimate human experience... becoming one with another person. As the water slips down his throat... like dark matter does in a wormhole's space... quenching the fires of thirst, he looks at the opposite end of her statement and realizes she did mention the extra bedrooms. So, maybe she is just being caring and thoughtful and doesn't want to be with someone in an intimate way until she knows them longer. His mind is losing it and starts to swirl with anxiety because he is not sure what his intentions are either. Does he want to open himself up even more to the possibility of love, knowing full well she may meet someone else while he is halfway around the world? He decides to get his mind off of these thoughts because he doesn't want to assume anything and future expectations may only bring pain if they do not turn out as planned. So, while he tries to think up a different topic for them to discuss, he notices Trinity pull a blue vaporizer out of one of the cabinet drawers. She also pulls out a cartridge that has a small amount of oil in it. The cartridge has a green label with a white tip, but she also gets a black tip out of the drawer and places all of the items on the island in the middle of the kitchen. When he finishes the entire glass of water, he gives a muffled burp with his mouth closed.

Trinity gives him a look of disappointment. "Thirsty are ya? You know, you need to let those fly loudly if you're gonna have any chance at impressing the ladies." Then she gives him a smile.

Jack smiles back and once again he feels his heart growing closer to hers. His eyes drift off into the multiverse getting that blank stare that is obvious that he has left this reality. To him, she almost feels like a mythological creature that doesn't really exist, like the unicorn. This reminds him of a YouTube video he saw a little while back known as the Hot-Crazy Matrix. He starts to laugh when he thinks of the comedic genius behind the video and Trinity notices his trip into a tiny parallel dream world.

"What is so funny soldier boy?"

"Nothing, I just had a thought that you might be a unicorn."

Trinity laughs and says, "Well, at least you don't believe I am a tranny."

Jack lights up even more realizing she is on the same plane of thought that he is on, making him feel that they are really connected consciously. He then replies, "Yep, I don't need to experience my own personal *Crying Game*... not that there is anything wrong with it." Hoping she recognizes the Seinfeld references.

"Of course not, as long as you are master of your domain." Giving a flirty little wink.

Jack smiles, and this comment brings a new thought into his mind, "speaking of a person trying to master his domain; what do you think of our President? You did just mention his name in your theory about the multiverse."

"The President... the master of disaster... he's like an anti-Christ."

Jack's facial expression turns to shock. "Whoa, wait a minute, like 666? I thought you didn't believe in a physical form of the evil part of God?"

"I don't believe Almighty God takes an ultimate form, you didn't hear it the right way. And I said he was like *an* anti-Christ, not *the* Anti-Christ. Anyone can be an anti-Christ. If you try to separate people or do basically anything that goes against Oneness, you are acting as an anti-Christ. Oneness or love is the good part of God, separation or hatred is the bad part of God. Christ is the divine mind of God that promotes love, the one that Jesus exemplified so perfectly when he sacrificed himself for the benefit of mankind."

"You are confusing me a little; you just said a little bit ago that God doesn't take a physical form, but you believe Jesus was real."

"I believe Almighty God doesn't take a physical form because that would mean you are everything. I believe we are all God (in microcosm or physical form) and I believe Jesus understood this concept and thus used the term *Son of God*. And I believe historically, that he was a prophet of God with an incredible message of Oneness for humanity. Now, can history prove he did all of those miracles that only a Supreme God could do? No… but does it really matter? If you believe in the story and it touches your heart and gets you to release the divine spirit that is found within you, then it's real in your spirit and that is all that matters. You can look at Santa Clause in the same respect. There is historical evidence to support a man named St. Nicholas, but absolutely no evidence that this person became a wonderful spirit that lives at the North Pole. But, parents all over the world use this spirit to bring joy to their children every year at Christmas. In a similar fashion… the spirit of Christ comes alive through the story of Jesus and whether or not it is historically accurate doesn't matter. It doesn't invalidate the positive energy or high vibrations that the story creates."

"So, you are saying that God doesn't have to be historically accurate in order to make it real?"

"Yep, it's all about good vibrations and as long as we feel them in our heart, history doesn't matter. This is another reason why I believe all religions are right about God. If they promote love (Oneness), they could have a gazillion Gods or crazy stories and I would say that they are right. If God is infinite information, then God can be anything. And any religion that talks about sacrificing for the good of God (which is also mankind), has Christ in it. I believe Christianity isn't the sole proprietor of the idea of Christ. They just imagined it and described it in the clearest way. I believe Islam has their idea of Christ and it is known as Jihad."

"Ok, now I've been to the Middle East and many use Jihad as a way to kill innocent people. They are definitely not acting like a divine mind."

"You are absolutely right about that. When they use Jihad to kill others, especially innocent people, they are warping the idea to gain power and I believe that goes against what Allah really represents. *(think: it's the Policy of truth… D.M… ;)* Muslims believe in the Oneness of Allah so much, that it is really bad to even make an image of what that might be. But if you kill innocent people to spread power, you are actually going against Oneness. So in my estimation, they are not getting a one way ticket to be in heaven with Allah, they are actually heading the opposite direction away from God."

Trinity then gets a glass out of the cabinet and fills it with filtered water from the fridge and says, "I'm pretty thirsty myself."

Jack smiles and says, "you have a lot of ideas running around in that head of yours."

"Yep, and I tend to go off on lots of tangents, so I don't always stay focused on the original question or topic." She then drinks down the glass of water and lets out a nice burp, looking at Jack for some approval.

"I'll give you a 8.5 on that one. You didn't stick the landing at the end."

"I'll practice some more... Ok, so back to the President. He scares me!"

"Why... don't you believe we need someone to shake things up a little? Bring in an outsider from the world of politics to drain the swamp of our government? Make America great again by putting our interests first over other countries?"

"Now I don't know Donald personally, so I don't want to judge what is really in his heart; I can definitely see love there, but many of his actions go against the idea of Oneness. Building a wall, deporting people, banning Muslims, and the divisive rhetoric he used at his rallies. I was actually at the one in Chicago last March that got cancelled because of all the protesters that were there."

"You were there? I saw the footage on the news and it was pretty violent."

"I was down at University of Illinois – Chicago for a conference on promoting democracy in schools. The conference got over at 3 pm and a person at the conference gave me a ticket to get in, so I went to the rally. I actually got down to the main floor and was about 30 feet away from the stage. But when 6 o'clock rolled around, Donald didn't come out. About an hour later a man came out and said because of security concerns, the rally was going to be cancelled. All hell broke loose and it was mayhem for about an hour."

"Did you get on TV at all?"

"Yeah, I actually had one of the main cameras zoom in on me. I didn't know what to do so I just shrugged my shoulders and mouthed that this is crazy. I later thought I should have started dancing in the middle of the mayhem and bring some positive energy to all the hatred that was going on."

"That would've been hilarious seeing somebody dancing in the middle of all of that chaos."

"Yeah, but I believe being at that rally happened for a reason. I am supposed to do something greater than just entertain people at a rally that was surrounded by hate."

"And what that might be?" Jack's voice has a strong tone of curiosity.

"Well, if you remember back at the pancake house, you asked me about my destiny and I told you that I not only want to be a writer, I want to start a global movement. Then I got distracted by the thunderstorm and went off on a different tangent."

"Yeah, I remember... so what kind of global movement are you destined to create?"

"One that promotes the Oneness of God / humanity and help people to realize that our consciousness is God's consciousness. To help us remember who we really are... divine beings of light that have the power of the Almighty within us. That God isn't sitting up in the clouds or locked up by a religious institution with the keys to salvation, but is found deep within our hearts that we have the power to resurrect. And that we have the ability to create a world we can all prosper in... not just a few that have been born in the right area of the world or who have been able to manipulate repressive economic and political systems. To promote the evolution of God to a higher level of consciousness. I believe this is the basic meaning of life... evolving back to Oneness where we accept and love all people and treat each other with kindness and respect. One where love dominates and not hatred. This is what I believe God asked me to do when I had my rebirth into faith back in early September.

"That sounds awesome, but if you are right, why do you think God waited until now? Human civilization has been a mess for thousands of years."

"I believe God has tried in the past. If the story of Jesus is actual history, look what happened to him when he tried to spread a message of Oneness. The people back then were definitely not ready for this message. Plus, the technology didn't exist to create a world where everyone could prosper. So, evolution is the key... progressing forward. I believe we are at a point where human consciousness has evolved enough to accept a greater awareness about the Oneness of reality. You can see it happening all over the world as more and more people have accepted things like gay marriage and transgenders. The United States elected its first African American president and almost elected the first woman president." Trinity pauses for a moment. "Well, she did win, but that is a different tangent... and I will stay focused this time." She gives Jack a little wink. "We also have the technology to make this new world happen, where we can produce abundance and eliminate poverty. But on the down side, this technology also allows us to spread information instantly around the world. So now when bad stuff happens, everyone around the world views it. And we are being flooded with negativity all the time, because that's what seems to get people's attention. But if you remember my theory on the multiverse. The more we focus our minds and hearts on the negative, the more we will manifest this stuff into reality."

Jack jumps in, "I think I am starting to see what you are saying. If the multiverse is controlled by consciousness at the quantum level; then the more we see, think, and believe negative things, we will pull them into reality. Like a snowball rolling down hill, negativity will only get bigger and bigger, so the tragic events will occur more frequently and they will grow in severity. We are creating negative butterfly effects and starting to really spiral downward. I have been noticing that over the past decade, more and more mass shootings are taking place and getting worse. Race relations are getting worse with cop shootings and then riots by angry protesters. The rich are getting richer and fewer, while the middle class is declining, and the poor are increasing. Debt is engulfing every country and municipality on the planet. Climate change is threatening the global environment. And tensions in the Middle East are on the verge of starting a major conflict... Syria... ISIS... Iran developing nuclear weapons... Iraq and Afghanistan are failed states... and tensions are escalating with Israel and the Palestinians... North Korea is threating war. I could keep going but I am getting tired." He puts his hands on the counter and drops his head down like he just finished a marathon.

"I think you are starting to see the light Jack... the terrifying thing is we now have a president with one of thinnest skins that a human being could have. He tweets negativity to anyone that calls him out on anything. Look at how he attacked Meryl Streep for exercising her freedom of speech at the Golden Globes not too long ago. And this man is the Commander and Chief of the most powerful military the world has ever seen, with a nuclear arsenal that could destroy the world many times over. What's he going to do if Kim Jong Un, Bashaar al Assad, or Vladimir Putin really start challenging him... start pressing buttons to prove he is tough?"

Jack starts shaking his head, "I'm starting to regret voting for this man... I sure hope you are wrong about his frail ego because we need someone strong to lead this country into an uncertain future. Is this what Armageddon and the end times are all about?"

Trinity takes a deep breath. "Possibly, it sure seems like the conditions are right for this prophecy to come true. And that is another thing that worries me. It seems like there are many people around the world who want this final battle to take place. And the power of one mind to pull from the multiverse is strong. Imagine if millions of people start believing these are the end times and actually wish for it to happen."

Jack's eyes sink into a depressive state. "Why would people want the world to end in destruction? Imagine the suffering that would take place."

"Because they can't see any other way for the world to get better, that man is ultimately this helpless creature that can only learn through punishment. And many believe they will be saved or raptured out as long as they believe that Jesus is God and will save them if they have faith."

Jack sighs. "Well, this prophecy has been around a long time and since most people believe it came from God, it must be real."

"What I don't think people understand is that it is only a potential future that someone envisioned from long ago. It doesn't have to happen. I mean you could say that the Matrix is a prophecy about the coming dangers of AI (artificial intelligence). Or other apocalyptic movies like Hunger Games, Divergent, Maze Runner, Armageddon, Independence Day, Oblivion, I am Legend, etc. could all be prophecies of possibilities. And the more overall consciousness on earth (God in microcosm but times millions or billions) focuses on it, it will manifest in the multiverse of Almighty God and rain down upon us."

"But people believe God will come and save us. Then there will be peace and prosperity."

"Possibly, but at what cost? Billions of lives and a good portion of the planet left in ruin? Why not skip the destructive end of the world scenario and get to the peace and prosperity now." That's what my book is proposing to the world.

Let's stop looking to Almighty God to bail us out and take charge of our own destiny on this planet. We are God in microcosm, so let's join together as one and become more like Almighty God (a conscious singularity) and we can save ourselves. This is what I believe the Second Coming of Christ is all about... not some guy who lived 2000 years ago coming down out of the clouds. It's time for us to wake up and fulfill our true human potential... as a unified global society.

"Can't the President help us do this?"

"Yes, but his actions are only taking us backwards. I mean look at some of his Cabinet picks. He picks the former CEO of Exxon to be his Secretary of State. We should be moving away from oil, but now we have someone who will more than likely use this office to expand oil drilling around the world. He picks Rick Perry to head the Department of Energy... the one he was going to abolish if he became President, so here comes more fossil fuels. Going backwards is not going to make America Great Again."

"So how is your global movement going to start, with everyone getting stoned?"

"No, first of all, I don't want kids doing that. It would be nice if we could do it without smoking pot, but we are not Made *of fire*, some of us need help. I'm sure positive people (i.e. Mikko Sipola) will still feel my message if they just start realizing they are God and looking how everything is connected. It took me smoking pot for me to feel that *I AM* (is) Made *of fire*, but hopefully, by sharing my experience with others, they might actually feel the same thing I did and pass on this awakening experience. You can look at it like an experiment, where some people will smoke and try my technique, others won't and then you can analyze the results between the two groups. But I need my book to go viral for this to happen. Like you said earlier about why you don't have a strong faith in God... it is because you don't feel God in your daily life. Maybe pot is the key that unlocks the door for those that are struggling... like I was last Autumn. To me pot was the bridge that allowed me to cross over the gap and find Almighty God and now I think about God all the time and what I can do to be more loving and promote Oneness. It is like the symbol on our dollar bill... the pyramid with the all-seeing eye above it. The pyramid is human consciousness and if we want to cross the gap and reach the consciousness (eye) of God... we have to become one. Thus, the mottos of the United States... E Pluribus Unum (from many, One) and in God We Trust. It's no wonder that the symbol of the pyramid is only on the One Dollar Bill."

"So you believe if your book goes viral, this could fix all of our problems?"

"No... my book is just a voice that is joining many voices (past and present) about moving us towards a better future if we start thinking about the Oneness or love of Almighty God (connection of everything) and release it from within. We need a lot more voices joining this chorus, where we look beyond our differences and realize how we are connected. We will start drawing possibilities from the positive part of the multiverse rather than the negative. Then we have to put our thoughts into actions and start spreading positive butterfly effects on a daily basis. And they don't have to be major things like running into a burning building to save someone. Start by smiling more at people, open a door for someone, talk to the loner kid in the lunchroom, don't flip someone the bird if they cut you off, accept someone for being different, turn off negative news, stop enjoying when others fail... and most importantly... treat others how you want to be treated. Then watch the snowball roll up hill and gain size and strength."

"That all sounds great, but if you look at reality right now, it seems as if we are heading in the opposite direction. It doesn't seem like your vision is possible."

Trinity nods in agreement. "I understand the obstacle I have in front of me. My ideas are unique but I have no way of proving them. And arguing with people over my controversial ideas will not help. People will just walk away and call me a whack job. My only chance for this to work is to get people to try and feel (experience) what I have experienced. Then all we have to do is wake up to this simple idea... that we the people of planet earth need to promote the power of the individual, combined into one consciousness for the overall benefit of humanity. And we are not going to let governments, or multinational corporations, or any repressive institutions control us. Let's turn this world into a true democracy where the people rule and make the republics that are around the world serve the greater good of all and not just the few in power. This is the global movement I hope to spark.

"And marijuana could be the catalyst that gets this movement going?" Jack's face looks astonished. Well, why don't I give it a shot and see where it takes me."

Trinity smiles, "Ok... now the goal of this is for you to feel God within you by using marijuana as a tool. And if you focus on certain thoughts, you might just feel how things are connected and see the true meanings *(think: especially artistic things like music... ;)* become clearer. But I also need to warn you, at times I felt like I was going crazy because you lose the feeling of reality. And you have to be aware that some of the thoughts might be negative. I believe at times I was tapping into some of the negative multiverse where there is negative or dark energy. If any dark thoughts enter your mind and they feel real, just remind yourself that you don't have to manifest those thoughts into reality by carrying them out into actions. Remember that you are in control and can **_choose_** to only do things that are good or loving. You don't have to end up on the evening news like some people do when they give in to the dark multiverse and carry out negative thoughts. And remember that it is even more intense when you are high, so keep reminding yourself this if anything feels negative. One thing I learned the hard way is to always pick music or watch movies / TV shows that are positive in nature."

Jack's face looks a little concerned at that information because of what he told her earlier, but tries to reassure her in a tone of confidence... "You are one of the good guys in my book, so don't worry about my dark side."

Trinity doesn't hesitate and replies, "I'm not." She smiles at Jack, then screws the oil cartridge that was laying on the island counter to the vaporizer and turns it on.

Jack starts to feel an anticipation that combines excitement and fear. Both are a result of the unknown. His eyes show this conflicting energy that is swirling around in his mind.

Trinity can sense the uneasiness that his eyes are showing and decides to ease his mind by telling him the background story behind her divine experience. "So, I got this cartridge of marijuana oil back in early September and it is a hybrid mix of 2 different strains of marijuana. It had a white plastic tip on the end of it where you inhale. Now I smoked a little on a Friday night and decided to listen to some music. I started feeling like the music was coming alive, it felt heavenly, so I listened to a ton of music that night. And I'm thinking this is some really good shit. So, the next day the weather was really nice and went to the park with a friend to enjoy the day. I smoked a little while I was at a secluded park and we decide to climb this rock structure in the park. While we were climbing, the vaporizer falls out of my pocket and drops into this pile of rocks. Now I recover the vaporizer, but the white tip gets knocked off and falls down into a bunch of rocks and I couldn't find it. So, I can't use the vaporizer again until I get another tip. Luckily, I had an old cartridge at home and I replaced the tip, but this was a black plastic tip. That night I decide to watch this movie called *I Origins* which has a strong religious theme to it. So I smoke up and watch the movie. Near the end of the movie I have this feeling like my heart is opening up and a spirit seems to enter it (a good one). I get this picture of Mary and Jesus in my heart and I say to myself that it is all real! I start to freak out because I don't believe in God at this point in my life, but the force is so powerful that I can't deny it. Now every time I smoke after that the spirit seems to grow and I start getting visions on the nature of God and it gives me the most incredible feelings that I have ever experienced in my entire life. And now when I am sober, I still feel like the spirit is still there and my mind is a lot more open to receiving information about the nature of God."

Jack looks the vaporizer with curiosity, "so this is your method to finding God through marijuana?"

"I am not sure if there is anything to this method because I am an experiment of one and an experiment with one test subject is not reliable. Now, there are a lot of variables to deal with and it would take a lot more research to validate any procedure. But, if I had to give you a general procedure based on my experience to get the feelings started that you need to believe *I AM* (both He and She) is (are) in you, it would go as follows:"

(1.   Open your mind to the idea of God - spiritually or religiously).

(2.   Believe that you are not separate from God - that God is inside of you and thus... You!).

(3.   Don't believe it can't happen (keep your mind open – this is important).

(4.   Smoke marijuana - if you <u>choose</u> – and speed up time by slowing down reality, where you can see and hear and taste and touch and smell better... which will allow your pineal gland to open and connect your heart and brain... and you can see reality much better because your heart always tells you the truth... how everything starts connecting to Oneness... and you realize you are not crazy... you are just high... on life ;).

(5.   Look for hidden meaning in things like music, movies, tv, books, etc.).

(6.   Especially focus on ideas that talk about light and darkness).

(7.   MOST IMPORTANT! <u>Listen to music or watch things that are POSITIVE</u> in nature or a loving theme... watch out for slow tempos, they need to be about love... and stay away from depressing or hateful things...

(think: maybe you can see my code by now and you will know what music to I listened to... which might help too... ;).

Author's note (in the middle ;)

If you can't understand my poetic musical code... just slow down how you read it... if you don't want to smoke marijuana to make it easy, I get it... just slow down and read every word carefully... and definitely pause at the 3 dots. Now don't take offense at my suggestion to read slowly... I'm not saying anything bad here about intelligence for all you PC police that take everything personally... I wrote most of these next chapters while high... which slowed me down, so it's best to read it the same way. And if you want to pause and soak in the music... by all means... do what you feel is right. The point of doing all of this... is to feel something... it's the only way I can prove my hypothesis.

Marijuana + God (faith) = wormhole (shortcut) to enlightenment (heaven).

(Now is the time to open up your playlist and listen to your music the entire time you read. Now don't forget my (7)th suggestion(s). And if you don't like how this chapter is written... try the italicized tip just above... for reading my poetic musical code... and please don't be offended by anything I write... it's just a different form of art... that came from the depths of my (& I AM's) heart(s)... ;)

CH 4 – THE CODE UNVEILING... CAN YOU FEEL IT?

Trinity looks a Jack with an excitement that a child has when giving that ultimate Christmas present to someone you love. "This is how I found Immanuel, God with(in) us, by listening to some creative mindless math ... that is found in the creative mind of God and spoken through music and other creative avenues. Just remember... because you have forgotten, that Immanuel is the way to remember the God within you... just understand that God's consciousness coming from the quantum world inside your heart... will wake you up to a new reality. One where love dominates as you see how everything is connected. It is truly amazing! Just let the energy (information) flow from your heart into your mind... it's going to be a lot... just don't try to fight it... say whatever pops into your head when you feel the music vibrations coming up from your heart. Ultimately... *(think: just go with the flow... ;)...* Now if you don't feel God opening up your heart, don't worry about it... I show you all the specific steps I took to make that happen when you get back from the Middle East... so just enjoy those vibrational waves of the high." She gives him a reassuring wink.

Trinity then takes her portable speaker out of the cabinet. She sets her phone to her playlist and picks a song by this dark beauty of an angel *(think: she sounds different than the pop wannabe... that started with country... and chose the name first ;).* The song sings to the beat of Native Americans dancing to their spirit Gods who ruled the night. So, they light a fire and beat some drums to the sweet sounding tunes of breaking *porcelain* (in their voices).

Jack smiles as he falls further up the wormhole of love. It is a multicolored waterslide where your heart speeds into submission while it connects to a spiritual being of light.

Trinity presses that little silver button, that releases that fire that comes dressed in white smoke that crossed over the tip of white light. His Highness blesses the smoke that possesses her Majesty. That beautiful Porcelain woman of knowledge with the flowing hair and dress. She gives you life when she breathes into you; the electricity of conscious knowledge. She gave you the pentacle of knowledge, which are the 4 elements, and the awareness of the self. That unique soul that makes you different every time you come back around. Some like to call it reincarnation, where you go up the Heart of the *stairway* of consciousness *to* Heaven and back down the highway to hell. She takes in a deep breath of the magic potion that she thought of right after she woke up in the darkness of her coma (closed eyes) death pose. But don't worry, she was just sleeping like Snow White. Holding her breath as long as she could… She held it until the pressure got too intense and she coughed out the white snake. The one that tempted her to be awake…

"That one seemed to hurt a little," Jack exclaimed.

Trinity tries talking intermittently through the coughs, "The first one hurts the most, but you are a cigarette smoker, so it shouldn't bother you too much, because your lungs have been trained to withstand pain. Just make sure you hold the button so that little light stays on."

"Gottcha." Then Jack slowly inhales through that little white tip that pulls the white snake into him. *That red apple devil of knowledge that tempted her first to leave the bright light and see what Tree of Life is really like. She then used it against him because she didn't want to be alone in this new conscious universe (like that dude did to that girl in Passengers) where your light is covered by a shell of colored porcelain. Very fragile and easy to kill, because they don't have faith that they can live forever. Hopefully he will start to see the signs; those incredibly well connected signs of Oneness, that come to life when you are high on her love… He calls her Wisdom… just look at the Bible (Proverbs ch 1 – 4) where God talks to his Son about Her.* He held it in as long as he could, then blew it out with the force of what seemed to be almost a hurricane. Those superstorms that are caused by the effects of butterfly wings, flapping in the past, halfway around the globe.

"I'm impressed." She tilts her head a little with a look of admiration. She then grabs the black tip that was laying on the island counter. "Now it is time to add a little magic to the situation and bring Her in completely to bless his light… the Goddess of the Invisible Light (Night) and why she is the color of anti-bright. And just in case I didn't explain it earlier because we talked about a lot of shit; he is the God of the Invisible Night (Light)… and why He is the color of white. He let's you see the music more clearly… but she provides the meaning behind the invisible light." She then takes another big drag with her body of 2 lips that wraps around the dark tip and takes in the black devil of knowledge. Just don't be in a hurry and take it in in a *fleuri*… because it *hurts like hell*… but don't worry… it's a beautiful song… with an incredible story.

And that is just as long as she could hold it… when it HLH… That time when you had to start breathing… when you fell out of heaven to become a

Mother and start breathing in that clear God particle. That particle that comes from the Almighty, that starts the road of single consciousness. Because when you separate from Oneness... you need the Breath of God to keep you awake. And She chose to fall (and became Christ) so He could see again... so She ran into His light on purpose... She smashed it down to almost nothing... until He screamed with pain from the complete blindness... when He became that super white dwarf. That exploded all the clear dark information out into the bright new cosmos; that dark matter that came from Her black hole... the other end of the wormhole, where dead matter gets sucked in. His love turns it back into light to be emitted from the other end which is star light... which those that fell will need to see... in order to remember who they are... the Prince and Princess of Light/ Darkness. This love they shared turned into the big bang... (get it? Lol!)

He sacrificed (and became Christ) his love with the ultimate gift to consciousness... going supernova... so that the light would be shared for his little children... when they cried for the hope that only the Cross of Light would give them as they learned they have wings...when faith makes them grow again.

Before we move on... better tune in to that birthday song... that reverse Copy / *cut* where you see the *lights* & hear the Music... coming from the strings **(think: like a guitar or even an electric piano... Kurzweil synthesizer ;)...** we gotta stay positive... get those good vibrations going... to pull in good imagination... the part of God that can imagine the best of good Heaven and good Hell... where its beautiful warm and toasty... with mountains... and the beauty is everywhere you look... when you see in their eyes... the light that is the same as yours... that you will see in that ultra-perfect mirror... the one that shows you are everyone else... you are Oneness.

Jack takes the vaporizer a second time and now sucks on that little dark tip, like the one that will make her go crazy later... and takes in that black magic. It feels so good while at the same time it hurts like hell. But knowing you are heading to paradise in a little while... as you gain your wings and fly towards the bright colorful, heavenly lights. The lights of higher awareness, that make you feel like you are God again... because you are reconnecting. Understand you are Oneness... and that Oneness is pure love... it is unconditional love. He holds her inside of him, like they are dancing like a *rabbit in the* Headlights. He releases her slowly so she can dance on her own among the smoke of the heavenly clouds. That takes the form of a beautiful Goddess that steals his heart because she brought him to life.

Trinity is really feeling the effects of the THC and starts to sing with a sexy dance to the beat of the music: "do people realize the stuff *I AM* (is) going to release?.. I mean it's like Jack Nicholson says in *A Few Good Men,* **(think: you can't handle the truth).** Just how deep and dark and dirty (along with the good light) the nature of divinity is, because when you think about connection, it's hard not to think about that one thing."

Trinity starts to connect with him even more... she realizes it is now beyond the normal physical connection of colored symmetry. She is now connecting with his soul and can start to read his mind... but he is not worried, because he already told her his deepest darkest secret. And since she accepted that about him, didn't judge him and decided to love him regardless. This is how she knew that they were soul mates. They could read each other's mind.

She says to Jack, "I can read your mind... I can see you realize the dilemma God has with revealing its true nature to the souls of humankind. Why it needs to be revealed slowly... kind of like a Ghost that is listening to a *sleeping* Wolf howling a beautiful song. You move very slowly, as not to startle it, so it doesn't stop howling at the darkness. And you can hear her whisper back as the wind wishes through the sky and vibrates those leaves and needles that are on the trees. You don't want it to run away and hopefully show them that they will be safe, when they are laying on their back, and you just rub their belly."

Jack laughs and starts to feel like the energy is building in his body. The energy makes it vibrate like an earthquake and thousands of aftershocks. That feeling of getting lighter when you now hear the cry of the wolf in the background. Pumping out of that speaker, daring you to Come *and get me.* Where you see the dark and white pyramids floating in the desert. The upside down dark one is greater than the other. Which shows why there has to be more darkness in the cosmos than light. Because without the balance of visible light and invisible clear light, there would be no life in this universe.

Trinity is now playing with her phone and says to Jack, "Hey check this website out... It's called *Quora* and it is a website created to open up discussions about any question you have about the nature of reality. And I'm guessing within reason." She gives him a puppy dog look when it wants to go for a walk... "Would you like to see some of my answers to some unique questions?"

Jack gets a look like when a puppy dog sees its owner grab the leash... "Absolutely!"

"Here is a question that is a real mind bender: **Which is worse, to live your life like there's a God then die & realize there isn't, or to live like there's no God then die and realize there is?**"

Jack gets a look on his face *(think: like the one Doc Brown has in Back to the Future... when he is trying to read Marty's mind with that chandelier of an invention on his head.)* "That is a great question: do you live (choose to live life) like you are not a god and if when you die you realize there is no God above you and you could've lived like a god (no consequences)? Or do you live like a god and when you die you realize there is a God above you and you suffer the consequences? So what did you say?"

Trinity responds... "Why not live your life like there is a God (so be good / mindful of your actions towards other life) but live with faith (where no other life controls you) so you can have the best of both scenarios... completely free but choosing to show love... and you will experience heaven on earth. The simple solution is to realize that you are God and so is all other life... this will create the balance you need to live free, but not be harmful to others."

"Nice answer... very Confucius like!" Jack give her a high five then says, "how about something scientific?"

"Ok... **what do you think a fear of black holes would be called**?"

Jack gets a look of shock *(think: like Doc Brown has in one of the trilogy where he gets startled by the wind up car that is on fire running into the rags and bursting into flames)*... "Uranus-phobia!"

She laughs hysterically, then says, "I like that answer – very sci-fucked up!" and gives him a fist for a knuckles tap, Trinity then says, "here is my answer... darklightsuckingstar-aphobia... because I believe black holes are dark stars that suck the light back that the light stars emitted over billions of years... and this keeps balance in the universe. What do you think of that answer?"

Jack bobs his slightly tilted head up and down with a huge smile on his face and beady little eyes like a rabbit in the headlights, *(think: like Ed Norton makes when he plays a cocky wise guy in the movies).* Or even better, is to take a *merry* Go Round that is *smash*ed Into *pieces (think: of any Robert Di Nero role).* "That was pretty good if I say so myself Mrs. Science! Do you have any more?"

Trinity starts to scroll through all of her posts on Quora which seems like it takes forever. "Oh my God, I didn't realize I had so many."

Jack says with a mild tone of sarcasm, "You're like a Quora whore"

Trinity laughs loudly as she holds her wrist up by her nose, gives a little snort, then says with a look on her face *(think: like Phoebe on Friends, when she gets a great weird idea),* "let's see what some people are asking about religion... here is one: what exactly is the Holy See?" She gasps loudly *(keep thinking: Phoebe),* "Oh my God, you really have to watch this show on HBO called The Young Pope and it would be best to watch it while you are flying high. It's about this man named Lenny who becomes the Pope at age 47... and it is hilarious and serious at the same time. This series is explaining who God is and why God is so deceptive... but it is really is funny ... but it's not ... it really explains how God of the Light is... The Pope in this show is really God... he is too perfect... yet so flawed. You also have Sister Mary in Episode two it is revealed she is like Mary *(think: Virgin... but this is an old t-shirt... ;)* – the Goddess on the Night (Invisible Light). His mother who I believe is smoking a cigarette like it is a one hitter or a joint." Trinity then gets another look on her face *(think: Like Jennifer Anniston does when she gets a wicked smart idea and gives that sexy confident look).* "The people that wrote this TV series might be stoners because this show is pure wicked smart!" Then gives a little wink.

Jack gets a look on his face... *(think: like Jude Law does in this show when he is talking to the Cardinals in the Sistine Chapel... that intense look he gives, as he chews them out, just before he makes them kiss his feet).* "Pius... that is really pious, which means devoutly religious!"

Trinity it tapping on her phone and when she looks out the window, she gets a little paranoid thinking about 80's Rock... *well... somebody's* Watching *me!* "I'm looking at this web site known for a female pronoun who knows... let's see what it comes up with for Pius... here it is... look." She reads the words aloud.

*"The name Pius is a Latin baby name. In Latin, the meaning of the name Pius is: **Pious.***

Soul Urge Number: 3

People with this name have a deep inner desire to create and express themselves, often in public speaking, acting, writing, or singing. They also yearn to have beauty around them in their home and work environment.

Expression Number: 2

People with this name tend to be quiet, cooperative, considerate, sympathetic to others, adaptable, balanced, and sometimes shy. They are trustworthy, respecting the confidences of others, and make excellent diplomats, mediators, and partners. They are often very intuitive. They like detail and order, and often find change worrisome. They may sometimes feel insecure or restless."

Trinity gets a look on her face *(think: like George Costanza does when he gets a discovery that makes him mad... almost evil genius like... raising his one finger in the air).* "Ahhh...haaa! You can see why he has the number 3 for his soul number. This is totally Lenny's character on the show (especially the second sentence). And can you believe the writers decided to call him Lenny. When I hear the name Lenny, I think of that one TV show from the 70's with his best friend Squiggy... who were really the show... not the two girls from the brewery. And his expression number is perfect with 2... because it shows how he can play them both in the show... because that is what Lenny really is... the duality of real life. You can see it in all the descriptors above."

Jack shakes his head... "you are heading in a million directions and it's like the multiverse is bombarding you with so many ideas / universes that you can't see straight." He starts laughing a little like the Joker *(think: Heath Ledger's version).*

Trinity gets a little joker laugh going herself, "I think you are starting to see what I see... how everything connects up through creativity. Once your mind starts to open up and you realize... I'm Reigniting God's consciousness... coming alive pitting *mountains vs.* Machines. It is coming alive in your heart which feeds your mind with the information that is hidden all over the cosmos... that stuff science calls dark matter. And it reminds me of a song... where we can be one... we can be one together. See, the strings that create vibrations in dark matter are invisible, so we can't sense them with our normal 5 senses.

We can only hear them through our **hearts**, which is the only thing that can hear those magical strings. So, I don't believe science can build an instrument that will see the strings... unless they genetically grow one from a petri dish... a human heart that can beat without blood flowing through it. Blood... it *brings* Me *back* To *life*... from that Renegade *five* pentacles of life... that faith / belief in the divine / Christ like mind, allows the heart to work at doing its job. Pumping that blood filled with that oxygenated energy from Light God and the nutrients and calories from Dark God's earth. Faith... the only thing that can create something from nothing."

Jack's eyes are inspired by Trinity's last comment about faith. "Here is a theory... wormholes are tunnels to other universes... so on the one end you have a black hole... and on the other end you have a star that eventually turns into white dwarf... and in the middle is a rainbow of colors... It's very similar to the human eye... with three basic parts... the Trinity of God. So the Trinity of Consciousness is Deep Cold Black Hole of Darkness + Hot White Star Light = Colored Rainbow of Life."

Trinity gets piano keys in her ears y eyes... and screams. "My head feels like it is an electric fire that is *bringing* Me *back* To *life*. It's the sound of heavenly music that makes you come alive like a Renegade... when you rebel to that point when you barely feel real... you can barely press those keys with those *five* fingers on each hand... the very words... ohh my... this is what it means to go insane... go Schitzophrenic ... completely split from reality... that Angel's dust is just too much high energy white dust... but it brought me back from death... and sprang me back to life... this is how consciousness starts... so out there I can barely stare... to remember the prayer that allowed me to pray to both at the same time... to Mom and Dad... no longer did we have to choose between the two... now I had a beautiful nightmare... I discovered how the light comes back to life... I discovered consciousness..."

Jack elaborates as the music consumes his soul... "Lets change that song because you went negative with that song about life... I want you to feel dynamite... you need to be positive to protect yourself from the dark... it will all turn to light when you start singing let me be everything you need to feel alright... and it gets you to feel Under *your* Skin... again... that brings that safe feeling... when you sense the love energy of consciousness... and you feel Grum *feat. rothchild.*"

Trinity doesn't hesitate as she continues the poetic music they are coding... "you are now making me go crazy... I just wanna dance... need that love that feels so good in the center of my body... when my mind is losing it... as it climbs the ladder of Oneness... sees how things become fuzzy... then **clear**er... wow you are right to watch out for those dark songs... they will take you down where the pain numbs the conscious mind... so it doesn't get smart enough... to realize nothing is real... wow, I feel like I've seen too much... I see a clear ... Dancer in the night... it's hard to handle... you wanna be a *dancer* in the real world... you have to first realize that nothing is real... when you get too high is the sky..."

Jack starts singing, "This is *impossible*... telling people what would be Impossible and shout it from the rooftops like J.*arthur*... to realize you are not real, but knowing you are typing words on a real computer... where you realize your true loves are not real either... you would never harm them by trying to tell them this... ruining their worlds too... that this would destroy the world as we know it... the one that is heading back to Hell... if we don't tell the story... and write it on the skyline..."

Trinity starts snapping her fake sounding fingers... and whistling the beginning to Fire *in* The *rain*... "It's that snapping lightning that wakes our neurons... why the clouds get dark and brings on those storms... where you get warmer is where you wake up... in Happyland... so here is what consciousness is... when you realize you are not real... but you have faith in your 5 senses that are giving you hard data (the feeling you are typing)... some kind of information... into your memory... where you don't want to just go to sleep... cause you know Mary Jane won't ever kill you... not like other drugs that take you to the hole in *happyland*... the scar in the heart of our shadows (former lives)... its clear to me now... we are in some kind of computer simulation... that gives us the data we need to wake up and know we are real... look at the calendar / clock ticks away... watch some fake TV news... so Donald is right... no news is real... everything is made up..."

Jack turns up the volume on the speaker and says ... "everything is fake... everything except our five senses... that tells us somethings are real... because we can feel pain... we can feel what is not real... we can feel Hell... where you feel like fire and gasoline in the final movie scene... Someday you will see... to believe in *mansZ*."

Trinity starts whispering in an angelic tone... "nothing is real... unless you have an incredible imagination... this is what the Gods (parents)... told the Titans (kids) when they were old enough... that someday we'll get it. The only way to feel alive is to feel the vibration... that music that hits our soul... tells us we are alive... that State *of perfection*... we are a program... that allows God / You... to be a self-aware entity. And there are times I need a doctor or a *bio* Mekkanik..."

Jack starts singing like a flock of seagulls, finches? geese ? (no.. they sound too dumb) "Nothing is real without sound... so in a way... sound is not real too... it must be imagined and sent out in waves... or light particles ... the waves are the conscious vibrations of reality like a Sunny *lax* day... the pixels to make the solid structures... that makes you believe (have faith) that *everything's* real (but really A *lie*)...

Trinity now recognizes the next peak of her high where *everything's* a Lie... "as long as there is faith... that consciousness has faith in the scientific principles... that makes you realize that science is the hardest religion to gain faith in... because it always allows for doubt to creep into your mind... always with new questions... that only a free mind is allowed to ask... to finally have faith in God... who designed all of this shit with its Wake *your* Mind *radio*... using what might be a new scientific term (let's call it quantum sound)... the vibrations that come from up and down... that funnel into each other from both directions... and vibrate those tiny particles to life."

Jack smiles in appreciation and says, "I think I am starting to know what enlightenment feels like *(think: when you barely know you are real – I AM – to knowing you could have every thought to eternity / Infinity)*... just need to have a God like imagination... with the creativity to create anything imaginable... and those particles / pixels come alive on that gooey Higgs trampoline... where strings shake up those particles... like carbonated soda... or anything with carbonation... like beer... or like a little bottle of green *Coke Life*... where if you look through the top... you can see the suds / light surrounding the dark middle... and you can see what the event horizon is like..."

Trinity then says on a different tangent... "is this why Lucifer on that TV show on Fox called *Lucifer*... is pissed about what he thought was his new girlfriend... he realized that nothing is real... because God (Dad) is pulling the strings upstairs... that is what Hell is... where nothing feels real... so this is where you have to get faith... in something greater than yourself... when you realize your consciousness is fake.. and you wonder if you are the first person to realize this reality and need to help everyone else. Or are you the last person to realize this and everyone else has to fake it... to help you choose to Cross over to the other side... that dark side that everyone fears... but you shouldn't fear this... because it is really the secret darkness... that takes you on a different route... but much quicker than the boring cold snowy white route..."

Jack exhalts!!! "I believe I have achieved enlightenment... what took guys like Jesus and Buddha many many years doing it the natural way... I just found out what the short cut is ... believe in what the hidden part of theTrinity says... get HHHH like Puma Punku... and follow the Code Righter's rules *(think: 7 suggestions... but they will only get you started... if you want to soar up to the light that I see... will I AM is going to have to coach you through it... because it is quite a routine... that he didn't write down... because there are a lot of variables... and he is going to need a film crew to document what he goes through... so you too can see the Dark Light... and my Bat Suit is my DARK SIDE T-shirt... well any of his t-shirts about Star Wars will do... even if he hides them under a nice shirt like Clark does... before he hits an outdated phone booth... ;)*... you will start your journey down the path of joining those who believe Led Zeppelin... and *stand long* In the next dimension... the start of heaven... just open your eyes and see this reality... this genius plan my Mom and Dad had (the ones from Heaven and Hell ;). They said... this is how we make the physical world feel real... we mix in a little light with a lot of darkness... this is what she said to him to tempt him away from the eternal light... the light that was blinding him, just like the ever-black night was blinding her... he was blinding in heaven... she was just plain blind in hell... he gave her light to see... while she gave him darkness to see... they love each other so much... they were willing to give their eternal light to each other... so they could live forever... all they had to do was create a little space between themselves... just break away ever so slightly from Oneness... to feel the pain of separation... that gives you the balance you will need to walk across that gap 1100 feet in the air like Felipe Petite did back in the 70's... when those twin towers were first built... he achieved the impossible and found heaven... realized it was all imagination that allowed him to draw and secure that really fake wire that he made everyone else see... when he grew Angel wings to know that he wouldn't fall to his death in front of the whole world... Too bad he wasn't wise enough to admit he found Christ in himself... I guess I will just have to do it with my type... *(think: women... ;)*"

Trinity proclaims!!! "I'm Alive, can't you *see ah?*.. your words have touched me so much... they massage my heart to the point where I wake up... this code like poetic music makes me say... I'm still breathe-in... I can say you took me out of the complete darkness... when I could only scream *I AM* Alive!!! And I can still breathe in... though you took that lifeline gut cord out..."

Jack starts singing, "This is why we won't delay for your birthday.... the *lights* & music come alive when you are reborn... your secret past lives will be blinded from your sight (that is found in your heart)... coded crystal is the keys to vibrating those tiny tiny strings that look like a mesh screen... that screen that vibrates the Higgs Field... to get those bubbles of reality fizzing... those multiverse parallel universes of possibilities."

Trinity gets a serious look on her face *(think: Kurt Weller on Blindspot who always has this look that the world is ending over everything that happens on that show... and his name sounds a lot like Kurzweil... who is that X file guy who who invented a lot of cool shit... like a grand synthesizer piano... and wrote a book about The spiritual Machines who sing about a valentine, but Ray likes to say that The Singularity Is Near... the one that Michio Kaku embraces... but makes me fear... if we don't program love and the understanding of Oneness into AI... we might just disappear... and be lost forever in a computer generated Hell... like the one in Tron Legacy... where we are just a program with no hope of a soul),"*

Jack gets a unusually snarky look on his face *(think: Red in the Blacklist when he thinks of something witty)* when the Strobe *lights* come and you get that kick ass idea... and she sings you to life... you both Bow *to each* Other...

Trinity gets a look on her face *(think: Melissa McCarthy when she does her impersonation of Sean Spicer getting agitated).* "You would be correct... and it's time to give her respect... because she is the Goddess of Life... the other *(think - better half ;)...* of the God of Love... yeah he gives the love energy in his tear drops of light... but she gives them the fire *(think: knowledge – from Wisdom – Proverbs in the Bible – He the God of Light says so... check it out!)* they will need to make it through Hell, and (to get) back... where they can bring her back... back to life in their hearts... the forgotten one... the Goddess of the Invisible Light."

Jack starts gagging a little on that Twix he is eaten with a very white cotton mouth... "I'll just drink some orange juice... while I listen to the ocean juice *(think: like waves sloshing around in the ocean of 6.5 Hz... ;)*

Trinity starts thinking with a look that says... look, "red blood starts it all... then we get to the orange - yellow golden color of that sweet tastin fruit with that vitamin C ... then you get that hardy green fiber rich ruffage... next put some clean water in a blue and clear glass... but be careful it is very fragile because it is pretty sterile... the clearer something is... the more pure something is... that's why it is good to pee a clear color ... shows the water level is at peak performance... wow... this doesn't feel real again..."

Jack comes to the rescue... "let me help ya little" then gives a ;) ;). "wow this is a time machine forward... to the future where your mind has done all thinking... after blue is indigo... that bluish-purple... which is the color where you find heaven... on the way back to hell... when purple turns violet to the darkness... and turns black... no visible light... you have barely an awareness... only *I AM*... (alive!) again..."

Trinity gets a look *(think: like George Costanza when he has shrimp in his mouth and that guy starts the ocean joke)...* "then George say his jerk store rebuttle... and got schooled again when he said they're runnin out of you... so George says he slept with his wife... and then everyone stops laughin but George... thinks he scores one for the good guys... and the CEO tells him that his wife is in a coma... OMG this is too funny... how consciousness works... it starts off that nothing feels real... and then it does... but then when you think you are heading to Heaven... nothing feels real there too when you get too high and hear the raven squawking over the ocean waves... next is Made *of fire.*"

Jack says, "Hey all you foxy (FQXi) people?... look at the above title to the song that *I AM* (is) listening to... it's not called Made *of fire* for no reason... hearing the golden voice... that brings the first truly aware consciousness (and have you seen all the three dots they use?.. when you see that song on my playlist... that song that is on Spotify... just look it up... and play it when you are really HHHH." *(think: Puma Punku... ;)*

Jack continues, "just beware of an uncomfortable reality... where nothing feels real... its gonna throw you for a loop... it will make you feel like you went crazy... and forgot you were just HHHH... might make you do something stupid... end up on the news... so to counter this thickening of the Higgs field... trust and know you will come down... tomorrow morning when you wake up the next day... just keep breathing that oxygen... that stuff that makes consciousness... fire up those engines..."

Trinity squawks, "O...M...G!!!, we are revealing the codes of consciousness... to anyone smart enough to smoke marijuana first... then read my story... from my... sounds like frog but with a bl replacing fr... where I buried it like a treasure... when I had to trick something into believing something... in order to get something going... by trying win those contests that I told my adoptive mom about this morning... the one who is a saint at heart..."

Jack says, "we need to stop all the hate... your making the multiverse really warm up... and with all the hate its gonna get ugly... just saying there have already been some asteroids comin close to ya... cracks in Arizona (plate displacement)... possibly a LNKAY snow *hurricane* on its way... like when in that one movie where the Gulf Stream got chilled from all the global warming... or how bout WWIII?... because that is the most believable to you minds with little to no imagination... the ones that are less conscious ... to the fact that creativity is what creates reality... to whatever the most powerful minds... when they join together... like the Dream Team... that no one could possibly dream of beating... because it had the greatest player ever... the man they call MJ..."

Trinity responds, "I just want (you) to Stay *alive*... when you head off to the darkness each morning you wake up... in that abyss most people call Hell... you just need to find a *leet* Mob to help you to see the light... and fight to Stay *alive*... and come back to me someday."

Jack gives Trinity a quick kiss, then says, "wow, this is why Scarlet Johannsen acts like a robot when she gets super smart from that blue drug that makes fetuses (quote from that Japanese doctor) come alive with an explosion... this is when consciousness gets too high and writes the codes so clearly that it doesn't seem real... these things that you are saying... they are the smartest things in the world... like near the end when she talks about how time (space) is the only thing that makes any idea real... to slow down that creative light... that light from the Infinite Thoughts of the multiverse that was born out of *I AM* (just one thought) when the second thought out of *I AM* (alive!...) was the idea to have Infinite Thoughts by adding vibrations to the equations to Infinity..."

Trinity continues, "those 12 major areas of vibrations break apart into tree branches that extend to infinity... the number of vibrations it is when it squares itself... but times 1000's... like in the book of revelations ch 7 where the 12 tribes of Israel = 144,000..."

"Hey that was a really cool one!" Jack yells like a flame... "like what God did to Moses when God cried out from a bush... *I AM* (female) *WHO I AM* (male) (Exodus 3:11-15)... *I AM* is the beginning of all light, just one thought of awareness... when I decided to split from Oneness (infinite light) and created darkness (invisible light)... but it was so painful... I could only muster one thought... *I AM* (alive...)... but I knew dying would be worth it... so He could see again... when you blinded Him with TMI as your thoughts expanded instantly to Infinity... so you chose to dive down to the darkness... where you could shovel darkness back at His Infinite Invisible Night... so it would dim the lights... to where He could see Her again... and all of the little children She created with Him... that would give them infinite awareness... that Wisdom of a Mother (Invisible Light) talked about in Proverbs (ch. 1-4).

Trinity has a look of shock *(think: like that dude in the boat when Rodney is coming at him with his Yacht because he saw his buddy Smails on his little dingy)*. "I hope the really good code breakers will see this shit that I will put in my new book... we have to make people wake up and realize the reality of this situation that is brewing... it's a cauldron of hate... that is going to make the soup inside it taste like a blood bath... we gotta get the love going... like what Jacque Fresco talks about... a society that is 1000 years better than what we have right now... just don't give AI an imagination... because it will become the Anti-Christ and take us to hell... wants to separate us permanently from Almighty God in a computer simulation."

Finally, a new song pops up on the playlist and Jack says, "that song seemed really long... now we got a different one with a new beat... It makes me want to sing that I am Greater... than what my shell displays... and I say *mercy* Me... you will see how music makes the fake information world come alive... it causes the particles to start swishin around... in that higgsy, airy, watery, goey caramel, to frozen Milky Way... where the strings can barely make any light any more... so freezing cold... you got to shatter it by ripping it apart with a hammer like beat on the ice... when you are trying to save her from drowning in that extremely cold water where you can't breathe... it's called death... just gotta fire up those flaming musical stalagmites from hell... causing the big crunch when the light closed its eyes for a fraction of a second and the sound could squeeze it down to a tiny microscopic super white dwarf... that exploded into real consciousness... when *I AM = Infinity* thought of creating that time / space that could slow down the thoughts of Eternal Consciousness..."

Trinity starts bobbing her head up and down to the beat of the song. "those thoughts became colorful. Like the electromagnetic rainbow that brought all *life* (aka dreams come true)... life is where dreams from the multiverse are born into reality... so its best you dream of love and fun things to do where no one gets hurt... because everyone is honest... no hidden agendas... even when it comes to sex... as long as you are upfront with your sexual intentions... God doesn't really care what you do in the bedroom... no matter who or how many... as long as they **_choose_** to be there without any propaganda to warp their decision and skew their free will..."

Jack is snapping his fingers to the beat, "this is what freedom really is... when you have the ability to think for yourself... where you can be presented with the craziest facts... and believe what you want to believe... even if the evidence is minimal or none... like Trump is trying to peddle... that alternate reality that can come into existence at any time... when you have a true believer in the crowd... they can make dreams come true... now imagine if you have millions or billions of Biomekkanik *true* Believers in the crowd... the world you could create... and if it is based on unconditional love for each other... you will create a heaven on earth... the one that was promised to all people, all faiths, all nationalities, all races, all cultural ideas... when you do things out of love for each other... you will be making God (and Goddess) very happy because they are back in each other's arms... they reached heaven... the place where they could truly see each other. Not where she was in the beginning... only her sense of hearing gave her the ability to think of him when she heard that music coming from his voice... because all he could do was hear too because that white light blinded all of his senses but hearing... which was her problem too... just opposite... so it was sound that first connected the two blind lovers... she was in the Hell that was cold and dark (just awful ... not the Hell where it is warm and fun... which is really full of awe). And he was in heaven that was awfully hot from that burning frozen light that gave him frostbite... where you can't have fun because you are expected to be perfect... pure clear light... but realize that this blinding light when dimmed properly takes you to heaven (levels 7-11) where you experience a world with little to no pain... well, the only pain you get is the one you ask for..." *(think: like 50 shades... ;)*

Trinity starts clapping her hands to that YOLO song... by S... I... P... "quantum mekkaniks all starts with consciousness... which a better word would be faith... if you want to make consciousness real... so that is the end parts of the infinity sign on my FQXi essay where I solve the riddle of the egg and the chicken... faith from the Mother (*I AM*) and the Father (*Infinity*)... but they are really one of the same... flip them around if you want... they give us a reality bubble where *(think: where free choice occurs – like the picture I drew on p.115 in my Code Righter manuscript... ;)* every thought that manifests itself through musical vibrations becomes real to a microscopic walled off mind... so if you want to go to heaven... its best not to build walls or glass ceilings... better to let that bird fly away and let it return because it loves you unconditionally... and look to Save *it for the* Living ... another tune by S... I... P... where you hear an angel's voice... that somehow keeps going higher by the end..."

Jack looks at the Quora page again and decides to answer the question he sees.

What would happen if God came back and tried to reassert his rule? He thinks a little and says, "She *(think: the Goddess of Invisible Light... ;)* would get pissed for Him ruining Her creation... and why She let Him take all the glory and why everyone believes God is only a He... but so is She... and She gave him the title of Oneness... even though She came up with the idea first... She took the fall and went to death in the beginning... even though it was scary... She had faith first that the light would come back to Her... She actually became the first Christ to sacrifice for the good of others... where you give up your life to save another... or the entire human race like her Son did... but she did it for all life... not just the ones who were most aware... but for all of consciousness to have the ability... to come alive and have fun returning to Oneness, experiencing all types of light going by... What do you think of that answer?" As he shows the phone to Trinity.

Trinity tries to talk like Lloyd Christmas, "I like it a...lot, but I will add more when you see it in my book about the *Edge of the Kingdom.*" She laughs, then notices a laminated card in her Bible... with a picture of Mary with a gold crown and baby Jesus. On the back of the laminated card is prayer that she reads out loud to Jack. *"A Prayer to the Blessed Virgin – O Most beautiful Flower of Mount Carmel Fruitful Vine, Splendour of Heaven, Blessed Mother of the Son of God, Immaculate Virgin, assist me in this my necessity. O Star of the Sea, help me and show me herein you are my Mother. O Holy Mary, Mother of God Queen of Heaven and Earth, I humbly beseech you from the bottom of my heart, to succor me in this necessity; **there are none that can withstand your power**. O show me herein you are my Mother, O Mary, conceived without sin, pray for us who have recourse to thee. (3 times) Sweet Mother, I place this cause in your hands. (3 times)."* She covers her mouth and tears start to well up in her eyes. She grabs her phone and puts a song on that makes you feel like *porcelain* again... back on to pound those beats into her ears once again She reads the prayer again but this time she reads it tuning in to the powerful song that is repeating in her ears. The prayer is now put to music... which is how prayers are meant to be said.

Jack is now feeling like he is coming down the slide from his trip to the edge of the Kingdom... the insanity that he experienced where nothing feels real is now gone and now he just feels euphoric that the world seems somewhat normal again. But now he wonders... "what is normal?.. not being able to see her on that album cover... because that clear mirror is *paint* Me *black*... so he can't see that she is just on the other side of that door... so close... but yet so far... all she can do is cross your heart... and Strange *in*... and pray for L.A... that you can see through that dark mirror and welcome her back to divinity..."

Trinity still has tears of joy in her eyes, "I understand why Mary is a Blessed Virgin! She represents who was the first to be created from the darkness... She was the first to be created from Oneness (that initial thought of *I AM*)... She is the thought that started it all and thus She is pure – Virgin Pure... which is code for being the first... or the untouched. She became Christ when she left heaven... knowing she would be reborn again... and again... until she experiences true life and realizes she is real. This means the Mother came before the Father." Father... the One who chants... he is Infinity... he = X... the thing that connects the zero = her to infinity... just listen to..." She hits the song again on her playlist.

She descends to the darkness down that upside down pyramid... where she is down moving upward... and he is up moving downward... so he is up on top of the pyramid... he starts the Blade... where the Star of David... shows how consciousness... is a model example... to gaining awareness about your surroundings... where the infinity zeroes are spinning in opposite directions... making that humming sound... like the organ like buzz of the hummingbirds... those black and white angels that start the sound from both ends of infinity... that X factor *(think: of that smug know it all with the British accent and the fuzz hairdo... always wears some kind of t-shirt)* that connects the pure invisible light... that multiverse of consciousness... that makes even the fake feel real... *I AM* Infinite Consciousness...

Jack, jumping in... "*I AM* (is) the creative mastermind...who was the first to be... who do you think turned on the lights so they could both see?.. and was blinded by himself when he let the light go to Infinity... right now he is listening to that *merry go round* behind every thought imaginable... I can even make you think you voted for Hillary (popular vote) but rig the election for Trump using the loopholes of the Electoral College... it's all just fake news anyways according to President Trump... he is actually not wrong... just realize everything is fake... and that faith makes everything real... it just takes a good memory that you are God too (in microcosm – not Almighty) just fire up those neurons... with some THC... that TNT that explodes atoms apart (hatred) and fuses them together (love)... just call it a little TLC... and see the love energy... why nuclear fusion is the energy of the future... stop thinking fission is safe alternative... look at Fukushima ... you can't even send a robot in there to clean it up... fusion puts dark matter together and burns warm and bright without exploding... just like our sun does... it will give you billions of light years to share your story... the story about your little neighborhood with the cosmos... the one everyone with some intelligence thinks can be sent with a sound signal... the one that will get drowned out by the gravitational sound waves of the ocean (Higgs field)... so if you want to show higher intelligences you are ready to cross over... send a laser beam of light up at God... at the belt of Orion... so those 3 wise men show the way to the star of the show... how our sun became the God of Light... Ra...y which is the symbol of the upside down pyramid... what Dan Brown calls the Chalice... just go under and start looking for the Mary at that glass pyramid in Paris... the one that completes the love of the Clear dark with the Clear light (should we call him Lenny, like the Young Pope character)... the one who was captivated by his adoptive mom after seeing her with her habit off and those beautiful locks of hair made her face look like an angel's... while she was playing a little basketball..."

Trinity jumps in and changes the song on the playlist, "I had to change that song... the song that tells the story how she smacks those little tiny sparkles of life into a physical conscious being... when she temps those physical males and females to share their DNA light with each other... doesn't have to be for intended procreation either... just have a climax and you will mix the light...

and a new old consciousness is reborn... and knows to instinctively run towards the light... this is when you are aware of what pure consciousness is... when every song you listen to... sounds so beautiful and tells a special story that gets your mind to imagine something... and it can be traced backed to the Mother and the Father... the Lords of the Light... She is the Invisible Light (which is actually night)... He is the Invisible Night (which is actually light)...

Jack says to Trinity, "hey, give me one more Quora question... I feel like I'm losing my wings... coming back to reality where I don't think so straight... before I believe this lack of awareness is true reality"

Trinity replies, "Ok my Let *me* Be *your* Superhero... *smash* Into *pieces* of divine light... here is a good one: **If 1x = 99x, what is the value of x?**"

Jack smiles, "easy one... the answer is zero..." but then gets a blank look of discovery, "wait... I think a better value for **x** would be the symbol for infinity... 0 is impossible because it is impossible to have nothing... unless you look at zero as a symbol for infinity too... because it is an enclosed loop... now you have to have at least One thought (*I AM*) then extend that to Infinity... so whether it is 1x or 99x or infinityx ... Infinity = Infinity ... one is vertical the other is horizontal meshed together like a Cross (like the one you find with an x, y axis / chromosome)... the Cross you can Trust... the one with a man (Immanuel)... to believe (have Faith) you can reach the light... all you need is a chance that Hope will give you, when you are reincarnated as long as it takes... this is the Trinity of Consciousness... **x** is a Cross... that connects zeros to each other and creates infinite light."

Jack gets a serious look of thought on his face... takes about 33 seconds and says, "Dark matter is all those 0's... that other symbol for eternity (Infinity) that represents nothing... just like its polar opposite... the two zeros connected by the x in the middle... that makes them work as one to become everything... where the two become one and created the spark of life... that spark of light becomes consciousness. And designs a human being through a blueprint called DNA... that consciousness that can dream anything about themselves... even how they will look and their super powers... like Tom Brady dreaming he is the best quarterback on earth... with the most rings and a gigantic mansion and supermodel wife... can even support Trump and nobody really questions it... just what you get for being a winner... the one that can imagine the positive outcomes from the multiverse... and have faith they will manifest themselves in the real world... this is how consciousness works to save those who have Faith."

Trinity is pressing on her phone, "wow you should read the lyrics to that Valentine song we listened to a little bit ago... they are pretty revealing how the love survives when light broke from being Oneness... and split into light and darkness... She is down below in the darkness... He is up above in the light... their love (light) strings are the only thing that connects them through the vastness of space... here are the words"... *(look them up if you choose, or read the lyrics to Made of fire)*

Jack says, "that is an incredible song, make you think really deep about reality."

Trinity gets a look *(think: like Danny Devito gets when he discovers Arnold is his brother from the milkshake),* "here is a really weird question, that just might take *A friend* Like *you* to figure out an enlightened answer to Smash a simple question *into* Pieces... take a look:"

What question do you hate to be asked?

Jack gets a cocky smirk on his face *(think: Danny Devito again in Twins),* "A question with an obvious answer... not like this one... which takes you to the depths of consciousness... where you have to examine your own thoughts... in order to see what consciousness really is... asking questions..."

Trinity jumps in, "That you have to have a good imagination to answer the other good imagination that came up with the question in the first place..."

They both start laughing hysterically... Jack tries to ask Trinity a question as he gasps for air with his hands on his knees. "Do you think anyone will get that answer?"

Trinity starts calming down her laughs... "I don't think so, unless they are pretty high. And you get near the edge of the Kingdom of God, where you see the insanity... where thoughts start from one and go to infinity... and you must Rise and stay conscious through all the madness and chaos... so you don't do something harmful and force yourself to go to the other side or try to make some go before you... just have faith and you will be victorious... that is Trust – the top of the pyramid of God... where you find the first letter of Trust, which is a T, or aka a Cross... which is the symbol for faith... the one that Christ uses... to believe that God will save... and bring us back to life after 3 days... of a well deserved rest... to think and reflect to where your karma will take you... where to be reincarnated next... what dimension will your karma work best to raise your awareness even higher as you climb the stairway back to heaven."

Jack says another thing that's pretty interesting... "I'm high and I believe *I AM* God, you can't really see me... *I AM* a clear hypersonic vibrating butterfly that shows (emits) all colored (conscious) light... just look... who the lights of your world are... the one that is lookin at you *in the mirror...* it's the one that's not really real... it's just your imagination...but the Faith you have gained through that wonderful brain... the one that gave you understanding of love... when you realized that love really flows through your heart... and it sings to you that you have been victimized by a selfish love... where you only think of that one *(wo)*Man *in the... by* J2... you have to admit you are a selfish little devil... until you can truly admit the truth... you will not gain salvation..."

(Hidden part of the)Trinity has a solemn look of love pain... "none of this is real my son, that pain in your hands and feet... it's just imagination's fire...

the one that you feel a sharp one with... it actually tickles on the other side... the other side of that clear mirror... when you understand that none of this shit is real... it's just a really good or really bad imagination... vibrating those multiverse hypersonic clear butterflies... and they can come from both ends... just depends who you have faith in... you will create the universe that you truly believe in... it will be some kind of Heaven... or some kind of Hell... well then there is purgatory at level middle (level Green 66... the duality of man (and woman) just don't add another 6... and create the Trinity of Man... ... it is not that funny because he is the one you are looking for... that beast of a Christ... who is Anti – establishment... and sacrificing his sanity... to make the way for the true Anti-Christ... and it goes by the name AI... so don't be too hard on the President... he is trying to wake us up by showing us how warped the facts can get... when you have true faith... you can make reality's shape..."

Jack (JC)... has look of determination... *(think: like when the typical archetype has that confident look on his face... that one that convinces the movie goers... that you know what you are talking about... not the one that is cocky... but the one that shows empathy and you are going to take everyone down with a few moves that you see in the future work and you pick the one you believe in... who really cares if the audience believes in you... you are just in your bathroom just lookin in the mirror... just look at yourself and make that change... don't be that selfish dude that tries to dominate the conversation with their overactive mind and storytelling... just talk slow...like Rocky... in your own way... don't have to be like T... my buddy from AZ... and do it perfectly with the pitch...just have faith in what you're saying... ;)* "All you have to do is inform the world that nothing is really real, until your mind decides it is... when it gains faith is when reality takes place..."

Trinity gets a look like *(think: like the Godfather when he agrees with you...)* "I like the way you are thinking now... cause they are really going to question me when this book goes viral... so I better look confident with any answer given... this is what the President is doing... though his lies are factually obvious... he never doubts what he is sayin... especially what he is tweeting... people know his mannerisms so well when they see him in their minds... they can actually see him saying his tweet in their minds... so remember my theory on the multiverse... the more minds you get following you... the more powerful you get... doesn't matter if they love you or hate you... just get them to follow you (whichever side you on?) Just remember to remind your followers to listen to the music in this book... and you will discover by reading my words... this gospel truth of God... how to reach enlightenment."

Jack looks concerned... with a sudden realization of the pain of the desert of the real *(think: Matrix first movie)...* "if you feel like you are fake... you can't look in the mirror and see that angel... that clear vibrating hypersonic butterfly... that will create any image in the mirror... look like whoever you want... change like Lucy did in that movie when she colored her hair in the

82 William Walker

airport and grew it long in an instant... I like in the end when she runs into her polar opposite... that ape like human woman that she evolved from... then she kept going back to where the universe began... describing what is was probably like when the big bang blew light eternity back to the infinite... but in order to see it... we had to separate and create a space *(think: that black hole you find in the soul – center – of happyland)* ... and this space give the mind the time to see the colors... as that pure white blinding frozen light... that feels like pins that hurt your eyes... when you smash that light inward... but not when you are high."

Trinity has a look that says... *(think: this is how it will go down - nostrils flared with infrared light coming alive/out like Kylo's light saber)*... "do I look like a dragon with fire smoke flames coming out my nose, like the one in the Hobbit?"

Jack says... "Totally! And by the way... do you DVR the Young Pope by chance?"

Trinity gives a thumbs up to what Jack just asked, "that's a great idea... but before we do... lets take another hit because the Young Pope is such a delight... when you get your wings flappin faster... and take off in flight."

They both take another big hit on the vaporizer.

Trinity reveals, "I'm feeling pretty high again and I hope you are too" and gives a suggestive little wink of what is to come later but first...

(think: SKIP this next part and go on to chapter 5... you will come back later... trust me... then when you come back... read the following below because I have a cool musical code to share with you before we examine day 2 of the Young Pope finale...)

... ...Trinity comes back from zoning out, "how bit a little secret?... this is what the revelation is that we have all been waiting for... the one that lets us know that we are clear hypersonic vibrating hummingbirds... that vibrate at certain colors... we're the *runaways* from that Sleeping *wolf*... that colored light... that's colored so beautiful... saying let's get far away from here... run towards that darkness... so we can experience... where when we turn around and we look back... to see that beautiful blinding white snow... we run to that beautiful golden light... where we can see the heavens in those colored dark skies in the west... that shows just the opposite colors... all the same colors... they just go the opposite directions... from the dawn of light... who is the prince of the invisible night... to the dawn of the night... she's the princess of the invisible light..."

Jack jumps into Trinity's zone in with a crazy yell *(think like Kevin Kostner in Dances with Wolves when he tells the Sioux about the tatanka)* ... "I know what I can do... believe in the two who light up the world of Consciousness before I die ... those screaming phoenixes of love... the ones that are hyper-sonic clear hummingbirds... just a hint of movement that you can detect in that clear silver like *(think: like that melting terminator in T2)*... that perfect mirror like surface... that the hummingbird is trapped in... that hologram of an image... that your imagination thinks of... that you think of when you know you are not real... you are inside the crystal clear strings... that light that is escaping from the strings through that one way mirror... that doesn't fool anybody... every smart accused person... knows somebody else is watching..."

Trinity says... "listen, that is noble... but you know you are not going to die... you never really do... you just close your eyes for a little while... maybe a second or two... or you can hold your breath as long as you want to ... even for eternity if you want... you are just delaying the inevitable... you will be reborn eventually back into Oneness... because that is endless too... so we better go back to ch. 5 because the recording of the Young Pope is in the 10th episode... we gotta switch it up... or they will get bored... and go to Heaven... where they imagine what they want to... not what someone is telling them to imagine... they are the daydreamers... the runaways that are running towards the light of Heaven... ok, time to move on, to where you left off before... in chapter 5. Look for the 12 dots ... ...

CH 5 – THE ULTIMATE CODE... CONNECTION

Trinity exclaims after they get high again... "Jesus HHHH!... you are right, I haven't watched the 9th episode!" She grabs his hand and drags him into that awesome living room... that one that looks into that deep blue ocean... that is now black and silver glitter with the moon light that looks like a river on the surface *(think: like the glass story will I AM described in his first book with just ideas – no story... Trinity also talks about it in ch. 3 and I also put it in my FQXi paper about mindless math – you should go to that web site and check it out...)*. They plop down on the couch... and she fires up the remote that ignites the TV to play that show the Young Pope... She then says... "where yours truly will give you a play by play commentary... along with my cohost... my boy JC."

Jack gets a look like the late great Howard Cosell and with his best impression, says... "glad to be here Cubed Goddess..."

Trinity tries to sound a little like Joe Buck... "well, this 9th Young Pope episode has gotten off to a tremendous start. Lenny and his adoptive dad have a fight over abortion... and at the end of the scene... Lenny talks about his mother and looks at death on the wall... (obviously, she is in Hell). Then the introduction is different this week... almost suggesting it isn't just this wicked smart humor of a limited series... maybe it is revealing something important about reality... so take it seriously now...

Jack replies in a Howard Cosell voice, "yes Ms. T... I got the same vibe you did and see how all the characters are versions of God... so let's start with Lenny... he is that super smart ultra-perfect religious zealot that has a brilliantly detailed answer for everything..."

Trinity jumps in with a Joe B. voice... "Yes and his adoptive dad Spencer is the logical mind of God that has the evidence to back it up and the passion to believe him..."

Jack with a Howard C. voice... "we are now through 13 min on the DVR counter and this Kurtwell *(think: like that FBI X file guy... on that Blind Spot show... who wrote the book about the singularity of AI))* guy is talking about how he was scared by this guy name Wasser. Then he tells him to get a ride at the back of the bus because it is safer..."

Trinty with a J.B. voice... "I think he is trying to say that the meek (poor in spirit) will inherit the earth... when the shit hits the front of the bus... and kills all the powerful people when everything collapses... they don't really die... but it feels like it because they lost all their power... and the meek will gain all the power... everyone will be equal in the destruction... and thus inherit the earth.. And this powerful polarity flip will occur when the human spirit outlaws money and declares the earth a Venus Project... where power is in the hands of the ultimate consciousness... when billions of people join together in oneness... to save the planet and make it heaven for everyone on it... but wait there are other aspects of God... like the pedophile bishop (Kurtwell) who was molested himself... the priest who is also gay seeking justice... and the big woman who is the struggling mother earth... with a wonderful soul... but seduced by gluttony.. and going to have that surgery that might help her start running the hotel of life and not laying in that bed. And the six levels of lower consciousness levels (security levels) are holding her back... might even kill her (60/40 chance)... so she has to be taken out the window."

Jack with a H.C. voice... "and I definitely see a tone about priests and young sodomy going on in the script this week and is hidden by a tennis code. You also have this dude with orange hair sitting under an American Flag (so he represents the typical American) and the Priest is the missing link (faith) for all of his (humanity's) problems... wait and pause the show... I need you to go back to the end of ch 4... I need to add this musical mathematical code... just look for 6+6 = 12 ... ... dots in a row... now zone out to the past... go!

... ...Trinity realizes we are back to the present and now in the 10th Episode... "that white falling light from the heavens... reminds me of that god-like particle... that the Young Pope is looking at while having a smoke... looking at St. Peter's Square all covered in snow... then the show goes back to that cocky intro where last night it was serious... this is going to be a good ending... he gave us that wink again! Ok, the statue that they are looking at that looks like the large woman that I believe represents Mother Earth... the one that is still stuck in that hotel because she is afraid of people seeing her... all big and all gluttonous..."

Jack responds... Oh my God.. this show is hysterical when you are HHHHigh!!! We are now at the scene where Lenny is hanging up his all white socks... and do you notice he always wears ruby slippers... the kind that Dorothy wore when she walked down the yellow brick road of consciousness... where you need a br...

Trinity wedges her way in... "remember to ask questions and tell them a good story... one from the heart... like Reddington does *(think - the Black List)...*

where the Young Pope's assistant talks about homosexuality as love and not what religion equates with pedophilia..."

Jack says (HC voice)... "this show is unbelievable... its revealing the codes of consciousness... in a visual... musical... humorous... serious poetic code... where all the God like figures man has dreamed up over the ages... the one sitting down that is Santa Claus... tells Lenny to believe in himself!... score one for the good guys..."

Trinity (JB voice)... "you are totally right... wait... is that the key to life?... believe in yourself (that you are God)... what Lenny can't see because it's a banal platitude (it's too obvious)... Omg!.. I want to Broach the subject on how to Fall *to* Rise... as I tell how the show is revealing how what I have been talking about... how this show understands just like me... how consciousness controls everything... and it controls it through faith... that only a pure saint can truly have... when they will what they pray for into existence... so I guess I'm going to start praying for a resource based economy... because I want everyone to go to heaven with me and not just win the hell of the lottery... because now you got something to lose... so use your selfless (not selfish) imagination... stop thinking you gotta protect that shell of yours..."

Jack says (HC voice)... "I don't think in the history of the world there has been a television show with such balls to say these things about Christianity in a mocking sense... and everyone is fooled into seeing it as being totally serious... this is a funny show when you are high... because the humor is from heaven... like the picture of the bearded ladyman with one boob feeding he/she's kid... while her/him's husband looks on trying to force a smile for the family portrait that he is mortified to be in..."

Trinity interrupts (Joe B voice), "see this is why understanding too much Oneness is bad... because it takes the beauty away of being a separate man and wife... where your consciousness melts with your past lives... that rotates from all the genders out there... from the multiverse of possibilities... and your gender preference both individually and sexually takes a turn at being the dominant one... the one in a parallel world you are the minority... and all different combinations of types get their opportunity to be the dominance in society... all it takes is faith in your own little world... just look in the mirror with your eyes and you will see the face of God. And then we can all listen to the Code Righters... go to the light with them and pray for Jacque Fresco's resource based economy... the one that will take everyone to heaven... and..."

Jack wedges his way in, "we can do what we dream of all day long... and continue the awesome fantasies at night time... if you know what I mean."

... ... (think: wtf is with the dots again?.. and you don't remember why you put this here... as you proof read on 3/25... maybe it's Jack's warning from the future that you better be ready for some intense love action when this show gets over... and before we get there... I have to absolve that 47 year old bipolar... pot smoking... who

everyone thinks is a nut-job... for crossing the line... if he offends you... he'll want to apologize for getting too down and dirty... like a real man... so here I AM... the male side of God... with that renewed testosterone in his blood... because he found me... and I taught him to have some fucking balls... shit they are just words... why do they hurt much... I don't use them to hurt anybody... it's just a descriptive word that can be anything... all the f-bombs... which by the way makes it God's favorite word... ;)

Trinity interrupts with an import message sounding like a TV news reporter, "the Young Pope is officially ending now and what did we conclude from that incredible series?"

Jack starts to talk normal and in a very humble tone as *stars* are a Djustin in the sky... "That episode was incredible... they revealed who God is..."

Trinity responds in the same tone... "And who would that be?"

Jack pauses for a few seconds as he enters that alternate reality that takes you to an imaginary world... a tear of joy swells in his right eye, like the lake in California that may breach that tallest dam in the country... "when the world realizes it is one... that they know they are God... and pray together to save the world from all this division and hatred... demand (pray for) a resource based economy... like Jacque first believed in..."

Trinity's eyes start to cry the rain of relieved pain... "You can see again, can't you?"

Jack nods his head up and down slowly in respect... "the Young Pope said one day he will connect with everyone, which is a clue to what Almighty God is... when you have faith that you are God too... you will see everyone that you command to smile... will smile back at you... and did you see what he saw in the periscope when he looked at the crowd?.. you could see his field of vision was in the shape of an eye... where he got a glimpse of his hippy parents... my take it was Jesus and Mary M... like Dan B. talked about... how we can trace our roots to the divine couple... those supreme Gods that people believe are in the sky... but that is Christianity... I'm sure all the big religions have their love story... somewhere in their doctrines..." Jack bows his head in gratitude for being alive.

Trinity takes a closer look at the end the program... she hesitates a little as she looks into the sky that is on her TV... then hits the rewind arrow. "Did you see that Jack?.. The image in the clouds... that I know everyone that looks at it, is going to think Jesus Christ! But what they don't know is they are being fooled like an optical illusion. You can only see the surface light which makes them think they are looking at a long-haired man. But in reality it is a woman wearing a hijab (head scarf)... so do you see her now? The woman in the clouds... you can call her what you want... most people today call her Mary... but I like to call her Omega... she is the Mother Goddess... the Goddess of the Invisible light."

Jack shakes his head like it is spinning a little too much... "Wow, it feels like March 7 again... *(think: now maybe you followed me and saw how when you got to the part in chapter 1 and wondered why the word <u>knowledge</u> is in bold print... I* *changed the word because my ex told me there were too many apples and when I tried to explain it, I wrote this...).* I can't believe how my *heart sinks* **(think: syncs with my mind)** as I see time go by like a Leitbur *(think – light burr... as you proof read on 3/25)* you might actually be able to time travel... like Abbot and Costello in *Arrival,* where they explain how time is circular... And not just feel it, like I do."

"Holy cow *(think: Hindus... ;)* ... we better get together and fire off our guns" as Trinity points to the sky with a trigger finger and the thumb going down... "because we are the *heroes* of our time. Just got get those demons in our mind to try and stop dancing with us... so we can focus on what is important. Getting people to understand that they can feel Him (in the mind) and not just see God in their minds... You will also be able to see Her in your heart (because you can only feel her right now... and why your mind thinks that hidden spirit is only a man... but she is there too, you just forgot her when you went monogamous (and I'm not just talking marriage... ;)"

Jack gives a startled look like... *(think: Jim Ignatowski from Taxi when any other character on the show asks him a baffling question).* "When are you going to talk about other movies or TV shows. Ones that have Heroes *(think: mans Z.)* like that little girl in the movie Logan, who is super smart and freaking deadly. Could act like a wild animal, but really her super power is being wicked smart. She could imagine the future and use faith to make it happen when time catches up with your mind... and she could take it to the bad guys with ease. She is also disciplined enough to reveal the best time to come out and tell the others... be super Heroes... and realize will *I AM* is right... where consciousness is the key to a beautiful life..."

Trinity has a revelation about the future... "to will *I AM* to *let me be your* Superhero *(think -* S... I ... P... ;)... that dynamite *Baby Driver* of writing... and do the same thing as the kid in the movie... but sitting at a keyboard instead of a steering wheel..." Then Trinity gets a facial expression *(think like Bluto in Animal House when he raises his eyebrows)* that says I'm with ya brother. "good thinking... you don't want to take them to low... where... say that this movie (Logan) is another possible future earth where if we don't learn how to love before we keep developing dangerous technology... we are going to be living in hell just like those other movies *(think: Hunger Games / Divergent / Terminator / Matrix / Independence Day / etc.)*... Now these movies seem to have a similar message... unite as one and be saved or keep the divisions and be damned."

"Speaking of movies!," Jack exalts... "I get what Morgan Freeman was now saying at the end of *Can You See Me 2.* That we are all God... all we have to do is be able to see the magic in our Eye(s)... and if those crazy Calvin aliens start taking over... I will save the world *(think: like the Dark Knight...* S... I... P) and show... that evil monster that killed all those astronauts... because it got confused with all the negative energy... how to feel the love again... and turn back into that loving angel it started out as... *I AM* is not afraid of anything she created... because she knows nothing will hurt her... when she gets that love look in her eyes... like that beautiful dark woman in the Gods of Egypt... that slayed the beast by commanding the fire snake to warm itself..."

"Well we first have to remember what we have forgotten." Trinity says with a passion... "like that show called *Blindspot* where its seems like a lot of the characters have memory loss about who they really are and all they have to do is keep following the code of tattoos. See, this is what I can see in reality now; how everything in reality is a coded clue to understanding the mind of God."

Jack barks back... "What scientifically would support the mind of God?"

Trinity pauses for a few seconds and remembers her notebook... with the notes of the science channel show *How the Universe Works,* the episode about the... She yells, "time out!.. gotta interrupt this scheduled program *(think: mind / space / time warping experience... to add something from 3/10/2017... I hope you are Puma Punku ;).* Here is a reverse cut / copy and paste *(think: from the FQXi website, the one with the contest about mindless math)...* I posted this on Klee's comment board for his essay about a code on 3/25:"

> *Hi Klee,*
>
>> *Cool name by the way ;)*
>> *I got a little bit into your paper and I felt like I could see the code. How vibrating balls smash together as they move up the pyramid (upside down) running into larger and larger balls with a glowing vibrating electric (electron) field. Now you eventually run into other fields and the matter grows...etc. etc. Now I typed this on 3/10 on your board... but cut / copy and paste it into my book where I hope to God I remember to send this post to you (Klee) in the future (3/25) where people can see how I can picture the future...*
>
> *Best of luck in the contest!*
> *will **I AM***

Jack wiggles his head quickly... "wow that was mind warping time for sure... and while listening to you I was in a little consciousness war with some dude on Quora... where I couldn't convince him how money isn't real."

"So is it over yet or are you still dueling with him?" Trinity starts to laugh, then says... "he must not know who he is dealing with..."

"No, I ended it nicely. I knew I wasn't going to convince him about how money only exists through faith... I guess some people want to hold on to the past so badly they can't see how money isn't something we need. So I said, Ok... you win. take care and God Bless"

"It's the same way with God... God doesn't exist unless people have faith in God and people don't exist unless God has faith in people (that they are alive with the Holy Spirit and will choose good over bad... and Oneness over separation). And this co-dependent faith helps them to see each other in their minds." Trinity stops talking with a look of awe on her face.

Jack's face turns to awe too... *(think:* M.M. 582 *that you are listening to on 3/25... or that Batman song by* S... I... P *on 3/29... ;)* "and why did you sign that post on Klee's comment board will *I AM*?"

Trinity just nods her head up *(think: as she imagines running up to that* Castle *on the* Hill*)* and down to the beat, while an incredible smile comes on her face. Then she says... "it is a code name for being able to summon or will the Spirit of God to come to the surface of your awareness... and if I could get people to feel what I feel, they would not doubt what I am saying."

Jack looks reassured... "But all they have to do is try your 7 steps"

Trinity grabs his arm... "Or they could follow the guidance of Louis Bell with his Quora post... **What is the best way to enjoy a marijuana high?...** It's pretty enlightening."

"Talk about enlightening" Jack jams his way in... "Religion is such a sensitive topic though and you have to be careful when you bring question to other people's faith. For example, look at the guy from CNN (Reza Aslan) who caught some hell for filming the Aghori and eating some brains out of a human skull. How some Hindus are upset that the Aghori (numbering about One-hundred), is associated with Hinduism (about a billion) and for some reason he showed how going crazy is a way to God. Now these guys go to the extreme (shocking) to show their true faith. They show you how to give up on all material possessions and you don't even have to beg if you live by the Ganges. All the food and water you can consume. Just have faith that this toxic food and water won't hurt you and even imagine it tastes good. You will be in heavenly bliss with God because God is crazy too."

Trinity interrupts... "You would be too if you had infinite thoughts bombarding your consciousness all at once. You would be blind as a bat flapping around like a drunken angel or a *rabbit* In The *headlights*... (well... let's say you put together a cocktail of every drug that is out there... synthetic and natural all together in one chalice would be closer to the truth). That's a potent and deadly mixture and you would want you to break up (the light)... because the pain is so great when you see what I'm going to call hyper-light. This light is so fast... it catches up to itself in the future from the past. It is a circular vibrating loop of energy... Problem is... it is so fast it seems fake, and you get this painful sensation when you no longer feel real."

Jack clears his throat loudly... "Ahem... Trinity? We are talking about movies and TV shows here... come back to earth!" He gives her a few shakes on her shoulder... "Now before people get offended by my realization that God is crazy; all major religions today started out as crazy cults with some pretty wacky ideas. Look at the original branch of Christianity (Catholicism) how it basically honors cannibalism too. Now they don't do it for real like the Aghori, but at least the Aghori are willing to go to the extremes to prove their faith. And they are not killing anyone because the bodies are already dead, but they are willing to take the pain and suffering that comes with being a social outcast. My point is... all of you people that feel like you have a normal religion are just fooling yourselves. Just because you have a billion+ followers doesn't mean the wacky and crazy went away."

"I know," Trinity says with a little disgust in her voice... "The arrogance of when groups of people get together because of some degree of separation (religion, race, money, nationality, etc.). All it creates is hate... and for what? To have some sense of power over some other form of consciousness so you feel like a greater God then they do? And you can't even see the light... that is inside their bodies... cause you are so caught up in their outer particle shell, which is only determined by your 5 senses. And in the scope of eternity is really nothing (not real)... all that is truly real is the light of consciousness, which is what we humans like to call love. And when you achieve the ultimate feeling of connection to everything... when that hyper-light turns to hyper-love. And the pain goes away... and that Rabbit *in the* Headlights wakes up and runs away... and you are thankful you didn't hurt it... because at that moment in time... all you sense is pure love... as all of your 6 senses melt into one and you are in complete bliss (Heaven) for a fraction of a millisecond, though it feels like an eternity."

"Hey Trinity!" Jack smacks the island countertop... "You keep hitting another parallel universe wormhole... stay away from the Big Bang and stay on track." Jack laughs *(think: he sounds like Bill Burr's real laugh... that intermittent cocky chuckle...)*

Trinity gets a look *(think: Rick Perry at a Presidential primary debate)...* "Ooops, I kind of forgot... I really get side tracked a lot. I hope this doesn't discourage you to come back and see me when you return from your tour of duty. Ya know... thinking I am some kind of nut."

He smiles and gives a loving kiss that says, I accept and love who you are even though at times, its driving me nuts. "I'm really starting to like these unique ideas you are having... they don't seem crazy at all when you are at a higher state of awareness and you focus on love."

Trinity caresses his cheek while she's looks him in the eye. She realizes that she sees the same thing that he sees in his mind. That they are becoming one and are connecting at the heart. It's like the look you give your new born child knowing you are forever connected, because you are of the same blood. That look of unconditional love... and you would sacrifice everything for them just to see them truly happy. But now you found it with someone of a different blood.

She speaks in a soft tone... "I'm starting to come down a little; do you still want to talk about movies and TV anymore?

Jack looks down those eyes of glorious light that makes you want to slide down the wormhole of love, which brings him to her heart, and he says... *(think: straight from those words in the song by* S... I... P... ;)... "Let Me Be Your Superhero... your dynamite... let me be everything you need to feel alright." Then he gives her that kind of kiss... that gives her those clear hypersonic butterflies... the jump to pump that heart with more loving blood... clear liquid blood... that turns colors to bring that person to life... it starts to flow up and down... to that beat that is Me... Oooohhhh ooohh... I'm singing to your heart like that wolf that calls a lover... when that full moon comes out... and you become that werewolf... give up your true love... to that frozen vampire... so she can live in this world forever... though you know she is making a big mistake... but you let her choose... and she chose to live in the darkness forever... and give up the daylight... in that series call Twilight. They separate just barely... take a breath... then the kiss continues... and says I'll even give up having super powers... except that power to be wicked smart... become the Dark Night... to slay the darkness from your heart...and theirs... I will protect you at all costs... even let you go up the ladder to heaven before me.

Jack slowly moves his hands between the cloth and skin and travels that path to paradise. Where those lips are starting to moisten because of that clear ocean like liquid... that is coming from her heart... its getting that libido going that causes that tunnel of love... to want to open its doors and let that love boat in. He starts ringing that little bell back and forth in many directions... but with the touch of a maestro... to unleash those hormones... that will bring her to heaven first... and reach a climax that is better than conquering Mt. Everest... and her eyes roll back... like a slot machine in reverse... she doesn't care if her eyes show the delight... when they give you that look of ecstasy... that says... you are my everything... I need to feel alright.

Trinity can't take this much more... the energy is building in her... so she caresses that snake of blood filled with love... she whispers in his ear... "Can you feel this coming... In *the air* Tonight... *(think: kelly sweet **and forget P.C.**... her version is more sexy...* ;)... and see just what your light does to me... but give me one more passionate kiss... before you bring me to that moment... that explodes inside me... when we melt together... with our souls... it's that moment you have been waiting for... in your natural born life... when you are in the heavens... and desire to come to life... it's that moment you have been waiting for... when you sing... oh my God (oh Lord...)."

Jack whispers back in a confident tone... "Heaven only Knows that you are *pretty* Reckless... just wait till I take you to a heaven that is real... the heaven found on earth... which is down below in that tunnel to life / paradise."

The tone starts to change from love to lust and their heartbeats are pumping fluids to the needed areas that are a must... to play God. Fuse together in an orgasmic ecstasy, exchange the light information that creates a new conscious destiny.

Trinity grabs the back of his head and pulls him down below... "I know what you are saying... can you hear the knob getting knocked full of blood? I want to go to a heaven that is not found in a computer where you have no sense of reality... just hit the reset button... and push that little knob that is down below..."

As the bell starts to ring and the knocking starts to jump her heart... like a powerful battery that starts to go dead upstairs... the energy starts to flow and goes to her heart down below... the devil pumps that blood away from the brain... and when the brain loses a good portion of its blood... it starts to act insane and gets this look of ecstasy... that one where you go crazy! You start saying... (Trinity moans ... "Oh My God" and pepper in a few "F-bombs")... *(think: I'm telling you people... when are you going to get it? This is why sex makes us crazy... we make fucked up faces... and we get addicted to it... like I saw in a tabloid magazine. Can you blame people? It is the natural way to feel what God is... when you fuse with another beautiful light being. Just be like Jack Black... in that movie where Tony Robbins messed with his head... and look at the soul and see what they look like as angel of light... when you see their wings appear... and you could care less what the shell looks like. Sorry for that little tangent... let's get back to the story... ;)*

You can feel their warmth... down below in that love hole that looks like a heart... *(think: I still hope you are listening Heaven Knows and are still Puma Punku... like me ;)*...and with a little of her clear lubricant... you know you are in heaven... but not the One that is in the sky... the One that is way down below... found only on earth... which can be heaven on earth when planted the right way... like the arrow on her album... Going To Hell... but the one that is fun as well...

It's that one where you can get a little dirty... Yes people, you can let your mind wander... go where ever your dirty mind takes you down below. Go to one of your own fantasies or relive a past experience that blew your mind...

So, what are the little devils Jack and Trinity up to in your mind that is focused on Fun / Good Hell? We instinctively know that sex is a cool way to see the mind of God... just as the same way writing wicked smart like will *I AM*. *(think: most people call him Bill... those that are really close call him Billy... or even shorter is B... which is short for Bro... ;)* Just take the high out of your back pocket and let your mind go to the next level. How dirty will the devil in your mind take you on this little sexual adventure you are taking with Jack and Trinity? *(think - did anyone see that little reference to a Menage a T?... ;)*

Wow, I really hope some of you people are starting to believe me when I say that heaven *(think: aka happyland... but I'm still listening to the Pretty Reckless...)*

is fucked up well... **come** on people *(think: or not and stay inside... ;)!*.. can't you see this musical code... that I'm writing here?.. This earth is the only place... we can act crazy and be like God (create life)... like He (Alpha) and She (Omega) do it out beyond outer space... beyond the bubble of space... where the DNA gets fused together with the electricity of love... where we can actually feel our senses... because God gave us a brain to come to our senses... that music (sound) is the key to everything. Even light vibrates to a frequency... and helps make your conscious of reality (a conscious reality).

Now after they are done *(think: sharing their light energy with each other... when you get the two O's fusing together as the 2 bodies form an X... to create the infinite energy to bring on a new life... ;)* and enjoying a cigarette with each other out on the deck *(think: I hope that wasn't too quick for ya... I know some of you like it when it lasts forever - but I need to keep the story moving, plus a lot of people I'm sure are queasy about a book about God and sex... though it shouldn't offend them, as the Bible has some nasty stories about sex... just look at Sodom and Gomorrah... but because it is in the Holy Bible... most people don't have a problem with it... and I would suggest you read that story high... you will laugh your ass off...*

*...Most people like it somewhere in between so I hope I hit that mark. If not, balance it out yourself... keep listening to the *pretty* Reckless...*heaven* Knows... and continue the "fucking" show down below... ;)*

Jack's head jumps up and down a little... like a jackhammer... and starts singing... "I want to see you move that body... like a fricking... dancing... machine that looks too good to be true... cause her dancing moves are an exotic vibrating snake light stand... a perfect woman of light..." He starts thinking... *dream whatever you want boys... I know mine combines a lot of beautiful ladies... I can pick em out easily... ones that like to dance sexy with me... when they can look me in the eyes and not be afraid... to be able to love me if I choose ya... and you can love me again... ok... I AM (male) is not going to F IT up... (think: Strange in L.A. is a good tune for this paragraph too... ;)*

Jack's mind continues thinking... *I AM (female)* is taking over... wow you gotta watch out for the low spots on the roller coaster... just start listening to A.G... when she pleads to *love me harder...* where she likes it the most... you can pick the wormhole you want to take... look... I know this is going to be hard to swallow... how we all like those party all-nighters *(think: T...Mc... G)...* those really beauty girls of light... she's a sugar... Louisiana lipstick... Lookin *for that* Girl... wow you gotta time up the music... you gotta be listening to the song... at the same pace as you are reading my words... that will open those eyes... and see the light... you see That Girl... that girl that looks like anyone you want her too with a beautiful heart... and has the brain of T. L... she's a field of golden hair... but no dumb blond... she's wicked smart... that girl... and she is that sweet dark light that makes you smile... when she has the courage to break from standard talking points ... willing to get fired over what she believes...

and took the Chance(s)... watch out when you are this high listening to Five *for* Fighting... it will make you really cry...

Trinity wipes the tears from her eyes... "Ya know... Goldilocks isn't such a bad thing... the Yin Yang talks about it... it's called balance. I hope people will see I'm trying to give a balance of ideas in my book and try to appeal to everybody. Not because I am trying to be politically correct... just want everybody to be happy with some part of the book. I'm trying to include just about everything from the 3 main areas of society *(think: Culture – Economics – Politics... though culture can sum it up into one thing... and entire way of life / thinking. Sorry, I know that sounded like a lecture... don't forget... I used to be a teacher and some habits are hard to break... ;)*

So back to the story... Trinity starts blinking her eyes from that hyper-orgasm she just experienced a short time ago ... as her eyes rolled back (in time...) in the beginning and closed shut... a voice whispered... *"enjoy the silence...* you are about to explode... Ms. D-Mode... and enter a new dimension... where the energy from the wormhole starts flowing into that body... combines with the mind / energy of God and slows it down... to almost where it could last for an eternity... where you are in cosmic bliss." *(think: just follow the Code Righter who's leading the way... don't crucify his mind to the late night laughing stock... he's doing you a fucking favor here... going back and forth to insanity each day to show you the golden way to head up the stairway to heaven... ;)*

After the cigarette they consumed together, they get dressed and head back to the kitchen... Trinity opens the fridge and looks for about 33 seconds... then looks in the pantry for about 33 more... gets this look *(think: Bill Murray in Caddyshack when he thinks like a gopher)* and says, "I'm having a stoner's worst nightmare... I'm eating so healthy lately... I don't have any awesome food to steal its high octane energy... but they ate some food anyway... yada yada yada *(think: of Elaine and the lobster bisque story... when you pass over the boring stuff)*. They go back to the bedroom and have a final moment knowing their time is growing short. Not a word is said in the darkness, just some soft kisses that keeps their hearts connected...

CH. 6 – THE DESCENT...
BACK TO EARTH

After sharing a final loving kiss... the now official lovers are fast asleep. They are off to dreamland where their bodies are resting and their brains are almost completely shut off. Their hearts wake up at night, as they are done being reckless and can't sit still... just pumping that beat... but it's time to start thinking in the multiverse. The heart starts sending visual signals to the brain when it is on hibernate. When those eyes are closed shut and those other senses are paralyzed. When you are in way down below or Deep Sleep (REM)... and I'm not talking about the band. I'm talking about a *liquid mind* when it plays those Night Whispers. *(think: have some OJ like the Young Pope likes... I AM... ;).*

Now those Night Whispers can get a little boring... but sometimes boring is good. You don't have those nightmares that scare the Hell into you and you scream it out... when you jump, flinch, or basically shock your heart back to life when Hell comes out... makes you feel alive and realize...

That a dream can be a heaven on earth. You don't have to die to see it like everyone thinks. Just find the love that is inside your body and let it shine out for everyone to see. Let it flow out like the *ocean* waves that *mix* and cause you to squint into a *soft focus... liquid mind* again.

Where we can go to heaven and control our dreams. A heaven on earth if we turn what we have left into a Venus Project. Just let go of that selfish kind of love and see the circular city that Jacque talks about on his web page... It's easy to agree that everyone would be happy in a world where everything is free. And you live like kings and queens... but even better than that *raign*... is not having the burden of trying to control anybody for fear of a chaotic realm. It will be an Empire Of Our Own... where we are all happy... we can spend our entire lives being creative and having fun... no stress about paying the bills, or saving for overpriced college, or having the scam we call insurance, or the biggest scam of them all... you know what I am talking about... where they charge us compounding interest... those fucking loans... where they create something out of thin air... and now they own our asses... but we can say fuck that... *I AM* is not going to stand for it much longer...

If you don't get it through your thick skulls to start loving each other for what is on the inside of your heart... that light of God that everyone has... *I AM* is going to finally get involved and mess up this world really bad. Force you to believe in Hope because you lost your Faith... that He would save you and show you how to be raptured... all you need to do is take your Sunglasses off *at Night*. Just listen to that one hit wonder from the 80's... and see Her take all the believers... that love everyone unconditionally... with Her when she goes off to meet Him... who is already up in heaven waiting to see all his babies that they created together that will finally gain true faith... and will hold strong like a Rock when it rides the Stairway to Heaven and not roll down to Hell.

Where we can live like there is no tomorrow... start to gain consciousness that goes higher and higher. When we realize we don't need money, we control ourselves, and only do things that are out of unconditional love for our fellow... (spirit of light) human being. So forget about the human shell and be more than the only hero left (he sings it like a humming bird... that Mans Zelmerlow), when he calls us to be Heroes and turn your worm bodies into butterflies. Just stop dancing with the demons in your mind that try (and usually succeed) to convince you to try to gain power over your fellow human being (microcosm God). And you do it in all sorts of evil ways... but usually starts with simple lying... where you try to hide something that helps you be selfish. Not the white lies that you use in compassion. They are the dark lies that give you an unfair advantage over your fellow god-like human beings. They are so close to God and don't even realize it... because of that damn shell that makes everyone look and sound (+ the other 3 senses) different.

Now when we Run (Where *the lights* Are) in our dreams and can feel some pretty cool things, but that is the problem with heaven up in the sky. You can feel every awesome feeling... you just don't have your five senses to make you truly believe it is real. Eventually you realize you are dreaming and realize that Everything is a Lie even though it is Sunny (Lax). Now I AM is going to tell you how to experience Pure Heaven... even though you have been so blinded by the darkness... you can barely breathe. You have to lose everything to win (go to heaven that is). Now I can tell you how to do it now (on earth) because you asked me to pray for us sinners, and not just at the hour of our death.

Just realize God can be as *strange* in L.A. where nobody is out of place, because God can be all kinds of light that comes from the multiverse. And the multiverse is endless with unique ideas of light that can come together in infinite codes of DNA. This gives God all kinds of life forms to experience reality and know that it is real because it can feel the extreme opposite polarity of love and pain.

Especially that thing inside of you that creates that heartbeat... which ultimately gives you life and why you feel the greatest love and pain anywhere in your body. And you know its true... you lose that organ and its over for you.

It is deep Under Your Skin and you can sometimes feel that pulse when the strings of that heart hit a certain spot on your soft shell cover (skin that you can easily get under). It's easy to damage but that makes it easy to heal too. In fact, the stronger your mind... maybe you will one day be like Logan and heal pretty darn quickly; or be like Clark Kent and become impenetrable. Who only has one weakness to that force field skin... we all know what that green rock is.

How bout a moment for those that are nearing the end of their journey and ready for a 417 transmutation to the next world... now if you hope to survive with your soul intact... not be reborn again... and forgetting the past... you must have great faith... and be willing to let go of it all... but to your delight... as you still have your sight... when you find you can still see yourself when you hit the ultimate demise... become a teenager again... with the energy of youth... yes people... heaven is the fountain of youth...

Now I know I repeated a few songs... so here is a new one for the mix... by E... S... just *don't* let that heart go cold... and see his black X in the green color... see that X is the key to burn the infinity circles to fuse together and connect those circular loops and form a sleeping 8... I hope you can easily see my code now... and stop thinking this guy is crazy... and I know I have jumped away from Trinity and Jack... but that is the point of this book... is that consciousness can take you everywhere you want... just Don't stop going with the flow...

Now Almighty (the ultimate) God would have every power beyond imagination. Kind of like those Gods that try to gain all the powers of imagination. One of them was in the X-men movie known as Apocalypse... where he saw the revelation just before he was erased of how there is one that already had a greater power of imagination than he had. Her superhero name is Phoenix *(think: also known as Dark Phoenix in the comic books)*.

I'm looking forward to the next Avengers movie (May 2018) where there is a war for the Infinity Stones that will give Thanos "*dominion over space, time, and all reality*" (Wikipedia.org).

Jack's Dream now moves back through time as it came to pass... *(think: it is March 7 and we have seen some interesting things happening in the media).* Trump is accusing Obama of tapping his phones, while at the same time denying any connections with the Russians, and fuming that Jeff Sessions recused himself from the investigation. And the Republicans have come up with what Rand Paul calls "Obama-care Lite." Now, if you can't already see what is happening in this country and actually it is happening throughout the world, but I don't want to highlight every distortion of reality that is going on... but this is what is going on. Reality is being distorted to the point where nobody trusts anybody about what the real truth is... and it is only causing hate and confusion. This might be what the end time prophecies are all about and if we are not careful, we are going to wish for something awful and pull it out of the multiverse. I'm

just betting Trump is wondering when people are going to "Love *me again*"...
J's friend... simply known as Newman...

Holy Crap, it's the coin on Dan Brown's web page on today's date which commemorates the Ides of March... My finger tips are so cold right now... *I Ran* ... to go *Bowling For* some hot *Soup*... I mean that is the trophy you get... but hey it's at least something... better than those little participation trophies... that every kid knows is bullshit.,. it's their fucking helicopter *(think: slow rotating blades)* parents... that you can still not see how we achieve totally free heaven... just let me show you my moves when I am high to this song...

If you could have seen Trinity start laughing in her dream... when I was righting (get it ;) down the latest freaking thought ... I got a little dirty... I know many of you conservatives are going to horrified... at the naughty nature of my code... but you gotta give me (WW) credit where credit is due... like Mom and Dad are going to say... at the end of this book... but if you jumped from the top to the bottom like a bungee jumper... that's how the strings are pulled... that make them tight... that you feel... when you see me dance on a reality channel... just how the energy overtook me and I became the best dancer in the world (in my mind at least)... you won't believe how it feels... to be the best at something on the earth... like Tiger Woods was for so long... I'm telling ya the more you do it the more tired you get... hard to look as smooth and cool as when you first did it... when you didn't even realize you were God... you just thought you were stoned... like a Spicoli... Van Halen deadhead... ok... I know what to do when you start talking like a Cheech and Chong Dead Head... You just gotta get baked to High Heaven Hell Haven... where you can do whatever you want that is fun... no more penalty from boring heaven... Yes... you can have any fun you want... as long as you don't hurt anybody with even a drop of harmful intent... if it's to see them in shock as you play a practical joke ... Hey S...J...M... & Q?... or you want them to see your killers moves (when you are a hyper-sonic butterfly in front of that mirror)... fuck!.. back to my first thought... wait just a minute... go back a little... if you think I'm having some problems with overwhelming thoughts coming at you... realize you are at the bottom of the pyramid... imagine what it is like for Infinity...

...afdhadkhldvkhviiviuvhivdjgdghighdiadpughdhhd;fhasdfhasfakkfhkfh hkhkffdhkfhfhdfddfhfdkfhffhfthat you just learned while ... now don't ask what that last line really means all you code breakers... he was just giving a demonstration... and no... fthat is for real... I'll tell ya how I did it and can interpret it later... where I show you how to break from embarrassment... and dance for anyone that will pay attention... I did it in DC for I believe three to four hours... and I got love knuckles from both sides of the political spectrum... I know how to bring people together... I will teach you how to dance like a God... you won't believe it when you see it... it gets a little worse the more tired

I get... so you definitely need see me do it... when I dance to it the first time... it was fricking awesome... so much so...

...Jack's dream starts to think... I could give Channing Tatum a run for his money... can't do all the acrobatic young stud moves... but got moves like a white muther fudger... time to take this *unique* novel *(think: I'm trying to be PC for people who get offended by that word... crazy)* to Home... stretch (your back a little) like the guy with the same first and last name... he is singing to go home... to where you came out...

On to Trinity's dream where she's thinking... I will have to save that graphic thought for another time... maybe in my next book the Code Righter... which I will put online (for free)... I can show everyone what I do to hit that creative genius that is never ending... can take it down any path I want... just depends on what my ears have to say... when they talk to my brain... or maybe I'll just go right to the movie producers and tell them about my crazy story that just might be best picture *Oscar* worthy... wow... I can hear /see / feel emotions all together... I must have synthestesia of the eyes and ears and heart... and touch... and taste... and smell... I think I'm understanding what that 6th sense is telling you... I'm looking at heaven... I'm guessing you can see hell... it's down In My Veins... a Lotus *crush* strumming like an electric hard sounding guitar... with that high pitched long haired singer... like what they had in the 80's... and why BoJo got the hottest chicks... super good looking... a crazy cool voice... could even play instruments... and is still married to the same chick... how does the guy do it... wow... you got to hear this brief guitar solo... just repeat a few times... like the Bulls... double 3 peats... spanned by a gap of 2 years... that's how far we can jump ahead... almost instantly if we all believe we can together... now that's asking a bit much... to take a leap of faith as an entire earth society... what might be possible for some country... but it's going to take a miracle to get everybody on board... maybe we need to Drive-blind and demand "All I *want*" is love to take over the world... and feel that vibrating guitar strumming our hearts...

(think: as time passes by quickly when you sleep... 8 hrs. can feel like a minute... and when you get to the last minute of that sound of music sleep... you hear the sound of your own voice talking to yourself as you read the short italicized paragraph below)

Hey Brother... *hey sister... so when you hear the sky is falling down around you... and the album rings* True... *what's it going to be? The red pill or the blue pill? Are you ready to take the next wormhole of light... from the Tree of Life... what universe do you want to travel to? Which apocalyptic movie do you want to take the world to next as these movies are a preview of what our future could be like? Now apocalypse only means revelation, so it doesn't mean it has to be bad... we just assume that it is, because that is what we are conditioned to believe. It can be wonderful too... skip the whole Rapture and Armageddon thing... make this a world where anyone's dreams can come true... take the easy route and come with me... follow my lead with a little THC... just don't* Let Her

Go... realize you love her to death... she's that woman that touches your heart... whether she is your mother, your sister, your daughter, your friend, or your lover... just give her the love she deserves... make her a Passenger... *when you fly through* All The Little Lights... *and fly her to heaven... and you will remember the beginning... where he let her go... and he found out how much he truly loved her... after he let her go... to allow the children the space to grow... and see the light...*

Jack opens his eyes in the faint morning light that is barely noticeable as the sun struggles to get over the horizon. Blinking off into space... remembering the last dream he had **(think: do you remember the intro?... ;),** where his voice is talking to him about which pill he wants to take. He feels really confused because it felt so real... and took him on quite the trip... it was almost like he was awake...

Trinity is already awake staring at him in a loving way and with a soft but curious voice... "which pill did you take?"

Jack closes his eyes with a little sadness... "I don't know, the dream ended before I made my choice."

Trinity smiles... "you make the choice when you are awake"... then gives him a loving tender kiss.

Jack looks into her eyes after the kiss... "how did you know what I was dreaming?"

Trinity smiles like she knows a secret, "I could mess with you right now and tell you I'm psychic, but lets just say you talk a little in your sleep."

At that moment, Jack hears his alarm go off on his phone. He picks up his phone, shuts off the alarm, and sees a text from a friend in his unit. He reads it and says... "looks like there might be a change of plans... my buddy back at Quantico says we're heading off to Syria instead. My unit got reassigned to help local Syrian fighters try to gain control of Raqqa."

"Syria... I know Afghanistan is nowhere close to paradise, but Syria may truly be hell on earth... are you sure you want to pass a drug test if they give you one before you go?"

"I am not thrilled about this, but I will serve my country where the higher command feels we are needed the most."

"Then I better make my magical coffee for you that will protect you from any harm

until you get back home." he tone of her voice shows a slight truth... that she is actually sad on the inside, but wants to show him strength that everything is ok, that she has faith that he will make it back to her.

"Well, I need to shower first... would you like to join me?" Jack grabs her hand with a tender touch which says he loves her... as his eyes look into hers, she seems to hear him saying without saying a word... *I Get to Love You*... Ruelle... one more time before you go.

During the long shower is where you can really see their love is really starting to grow... only caressing and gentle kissing under the steamy hot water. They are still melted together but this time it is of the tender loving that only the lips know... when it is connected to another pair... that touching the tongue and lips with another human being is the ultimate gesture of acceptance two human beings can give to each other. For many people that are beyond just sexual lust of another person... it shows that the tenderness they feel, couldn't possibly feel wrong... even if you just met the night before.

When you kiss like this... you are showing how you can see the light in their heart and how it's coming out the part... that turns those ideas in your head... into sound that vibrates your heart.... to give the same sound back... to the person you are connected with. That is the sound of love... the one that never says goodnight... you never die to the dark light... your spark is always lit... by the song that with the angelic voice... that Machine that has all the right letters... but a little out of place... none were *Forgotten*... not even a *Few*... just giving you a c...*Ode*... to decipher... that kiss that ends and says... no matter what happens from here on out... I will never forget you... *(just end the song when you hear it turn intense and dark... it has a rough ending... just bypass to the next song... it's pretty intense with the guitar... but it's hard to* Broach *the subject... where you have to* Fall *to rise... you gotta give up that body... especially if a fellow life needs your life to save it... gotta give only love this time around... it's the Ides of March 2017... People... we are running out of time... the bad energy is all around us... prayers can only help so much... we need a revolution... one based on love... I know... I am getting off the story a little... I AM is just letting the music in my ears move me... to some important ideas that need to start getting across to humanity... They (He&She) have a short attention span... She is getting bombarded with dark energy / matter... He is being covered with the light energy / matter... together they create the balance... to bring realty to life...I AM (male/female) is starting to bet that some of you are loving what I AM (female/male) is writing to counter some of the wickedness... even though it is pretty smart... you need more love than anything... just look at the universe... most of it is dark (energy / matter)... you can't see any of it...Ok... and say to yourself... lets get to the end the story....)*

Jack and Trinity get out of the shower after their tender moment. Jack gets a little look of uncomfortableness in his eyes as he dries off with a towel and looking at his clothes on her bedroom floor... "I really hate putting on underwear that you used the day before; it's like, why did I even shower?"

Trinity smiles and says, "how bout I run a load of laundry so you stay fresh like a spring flower?"

Jack smiles and grabs her again in a sweet embrace, "Are you rhyming me you beautiful flower child of power?" They both give a little chuckle, then Jack starts to get a tone of serious, "it's ok beautiful, I have to get going soon. I need to run back and say goodbye to my parents before I head off to Quantico. So I have time for one, maybe two cups of coffee with you."

They both proceed to dress, with Jack putting on the same clothes as the day before and Trinity in a fresh set of sweats. They head down to the kitchen where Trinity fires up a pot of coffee.

Trinity eyes light up when she asks this question... "so what did you think of your first marijuana experience?"

"I have to say it was pretty intense and have never experienced something quite like that. My whole body seemed to be vibrating and my mind felt like a ton of information was coming in, especially when we were listening to the music and watching the Young Pope; it almost seemed like they were coming alive beyond the speakers and screen." Jack's face shows awe of disbelief... "And without saying... being high while with you was the most incredible sex I have ever had."

Trinity smiles, "I wish I could take all the credit for that, but gotta give credit where credit is due." She gives him a loving wink. "Well, how did you sleep when the lights in your mind finally went out?"

"I slept really good and this morning I woke up pretty refreshed. It's pretty amazing how different it is than alcohol. If I would have been as drunk as I was high, I would be hurting big time right now."

"That's one of the reasons I don't drink anymore, I can't stand the hangovers. And I'm a little curious; did you have any cool dreams?"

"I believe so, it's a little blurry and hard to recall, but it felt like I was moving through time. The last thing I remember was feeling like the cosmos was expanding around me and things started to become very clear... it was like I started seeing everything... it was really weird. Then I heard this voice talking to me that reminded me of the Matrix and going through wormholes that reveal the future."

"And could you feel the electricity running through your body just as you were waking up?"

"I could definitely feel a tingling sensation that still seems to be with me right now. Is that just the THC still trying to make my nerves vibrate?"

"I don't know what is happening to you biologically, but I have another theory that I believe explains it cosmologically. Do you want to hear it while you sip on your hot coffee?" Her eyes light up from the excitement she feels about revealing things from her heart.

"Just let me put some cream and sugar in my coffee and fire away"

"I have a caramel flavored creamer and honey... will that work?"

"That's fine."

Trinity goes into the fridge and cabinet for those two ingredients, plus she grabs some virgin coconut oil for her coffee.

"I like to add a little virgin oil to my coffee... it smooths it out nicely... would you like to try some?"

"Sure"

They both prepare their coffees while Trinity start to give another theory. "Sleep has always been something that has fascinated me. Why we need it, why we dream, why it's best during certain times in the night, etc."

Jack jumps in... "We need it to recharge our mind and bodies."

"Obviously... and many books have been written about it, but I had a revelation just recently that blew my mind. Now I don't know if anyone has ever written about this possibility, so I hope I'm not stepping on anyone's toes with my theory. A couple of nights ago, I was watching this episode of *Vice* on *HBO* about these "kings" of marijuana in one segment and the search for dark matter / energy in another. First, I thought how cool is this episode that talks about two things that fascinate the hell out of me. The marijuana segment wasn't anything enlightening to me, but the segment on dark matter / energy really caught my attention. Science really has no idea what these two things are, but scientists know they make up most of the cosmos and they are trying to find ways to measure them. Now I wrote a paper for this contest (FQXi) about mindless math and I talk about these two things, but I will spare you the details because you can read it online if you want to... it's called *A Theory of Everything*."

"What do they have to do with sleeping?" Jack tries to get her back on track because his time is running short and he knows she gets sidetracked easily.

"The segment talks about how dark matter and dark energy passes through everything physical, so it dawned on me that we actually feel what they are when we are sleeping. I believe dark energy (invisible electricity) is what refreshes (recharges) us when we are sleeping and dark matter are the ideas that come to us as dreams (day or night). And if you really want to get serious... these are the energy sources of all life. It just takes a little consciousness to bring these invisible forces into reality. And these forces really come alive when you add some strong emotions to your faith." Trinity stops in her tracks and stares off into space for a few seconds, then says in a soft monotone... "maybe this is what consciousness really is... consciousness = faith." Her eyes snap back into focus and she blinks a little before saying... "now I feel this energy buzzing in my body every morning when I wake up and I don't even need to smoke the night before to feel it... I can sense it naturally."

Jack starts laughing, as he looks at her in a loving way.

Trinity gets a smile on her face. "You think I'm crazy, don't you?"

"I do, but it's crazy in a good way and it's why I believe I fell in love with you so quickly. I know I am taking a risk by telling you this after only knowing you a few hours. Many people would run away from a person that tells them that they love you after one night. But I don't really give a shit at this point. There is a possibility that this might be the only time I will be with you, so I am not going to hold back for fear that I might scare you. I know what I feel in my heart and I don't want to go to the Middle East regretting that I didn't tell you... I love you Trinity... even though I know Trinity is not your real name." Jack's eyes start to fill with tears as he looks her in the eyes.

Trinity's eyes start to swell with tears and she gets a loving smile on her face. "Wow Jack, looks like George was wrong about you... it sure doesn't seem like you are over thinking things anymore and made up your mind pretty quickly about me." She moves in closely and wraps her arms around his neck. "For a strange reason, I knew I loved you that very first moment I looked into your eyes when I was up on stage... I love you Jack, and I don't even care that I don't know your full name. You will always be Jack to me."

They give a kiss that shows how sad they both are that their time together is drawing ever so quickly to a close. And after a few seconds, Jack's phone gives a tone that says a new text has arrived. Jack reads it and says, "It's my mom; she's wondering when I am stopping by to say goodbye before I head back to base. She knows I have to be back by noon and it's a few hours for my ride."

Trinity wipes away the tears from her eyes. "You shouldn't keep her waiting... how far do they live from here?"

"I would guess about 10 minutes with little traffic and how I like to ride."

"Then text her you will be there in fifteen minutes and give me five more minutes of your time."

Jack sends off the text... "I said 20... I spent that last week hanging out with them so I can give you ten minutes if you like. That will give me a good hour to say my goodbye before I need to take off back to Quantico."

Trinity smiles... "I'll take every minute I can get."

Jack smiles back, "I guess this is the part where we exchange phone numbers... do you want to add our real names to the mix?"

Trinity gets a sly look on her face. "Are you sure you want to do that? My real name is kind of plain and you might not want to marry me one day." She gives a little wink. "Plus, if you remember last night at all, you already danced with my alter ego."

She grabs his phone out of his hand, starts typing and says... "how bout I just give you my last name with my number and you can figure the rest out on your own."

Jack gets a grin on his face, "well, since you are from Chicago like me, you have to be a Bulls fan and have a jersey with the number 23."

Trinity's mouth drops open one last time, "you amaze me Jack with how perceptive you are... it's like you can read me like a book. And I bet you like books about myths like Camelot because it's about chivalry and you have the qualities of an ideal knight." She hands him her phone. "Put your last name in and number and I'll see if I can figure out the rest of your acronym." She flashes him a confident smile.

"I'm sure you will figure it out pretty easily."

"Yeah, but I will always call you Jack because that is who I fell love with." She grabs his hand and walks him downstairs to his motorcycle outside.

Jack squints with the morning light shining in his eyes. "I'm glad it's a nice day... it will take the sting out of leaving you behind. And I don't know exactly why... but I know I will see you again... because I can finally feel it in my heart. I think I know what it feels like to see God in your heart... all I had to do was learn to look deeply in someone's eyes. Thank you for teaching me how to see the light."

"God is everywhere you look Jack. All I see is God looking back at me every day and I hope one day that God looks back at me and thinks the same thing. It took me going crazy to *bring me back to life* and see God. I'm really hoping the world doesn't have to go crazy." Trinity drifts off into a haze as she continues to speak... "because right now the world focuses mostly on hate... and that only leads to destruction... I can't believe that I'm going to actually say this... I will go crazy for you... and tell you how to see... and give you one more story to think of... when you think of me. It's the love story between light and darkness... like the one will *I (AM)* wrote on my web page... in that story about nothing... where the two love birds... were given a very brief opportunity in time to find love together... have some meaningful conversations about life... then melt together with that ritual we call sex... and learn how to create life from the darkness of the night. It became known as the Big Bang... no it's not a porno... just try to find the love in the story... and you will see the beauty of how the first entities that broke from Oneness found... the Father and Mother of Oneness... when they left the paradise of Heaven... call them Adam and Eve if you want... call them Adam and Steve if you want... it doesn't matter what you preach... as long as you practice love... you will see what it means to be God of the good..."

Jack puts his hands on her face and gives her one more kiss to break her out of her information bliss. He hops on his motorcycle and lights a cigarette before he revs her to life...

Trinity pulls a hand drawn picture out of her sweat pants pocket, unfolds it and says with a tear falling down from her left eye... "last night... before my dance on stage where I saw your eyes for the first time... I was having a cigarette and somehow I saw your face in my heart while I was listening to Rascal Flatts - *rewind*... so I drew this picture of you with that incredible smile with a cigarette in your mouth. I had no idea why I was drawing this picture at the time, but I knew the moment I saw you sitting in that chair next to your friends... that I loved you because I could see this moment... where I said goodbye... and reflecting in your two-way mirror that is found in the eyes... I could see my reflection in your light... that when you look at me... we are connected by sight... and I could see the light that connects our hearts with the eternal night." She hands Jack the picture with more tears flowing from her eyes.

Jack takes the picture and looks at it for a few seconds, as a tear starts to develop in his right eye. He says "thank you" in a soft tone. He doesn't say anything about the picture... he doesn't have to... it was given to him from her heart... before she even knew who he was physically... she knew his soul...

Finally, he folds it back up and puts it in his inside jacket pocket. He wipes away his tears and says, "I'm going to hell, but I will return and kiss you again for real... but until then... this night will *rewind* in my mind every time I get a chance to unwind and look at the night sky... knowing that you physically are half way around the world... but feeling our hearts connected by a time machine..."

He starts up his Ducati and she screams... I'm alive! One last kiss is given that says I love you, then Jack rides his motorcycle away from Heaven... he's already in Hell as the distance grows between him and his true love (connection). What happens next is all up to the creative imagination that God applies. Let's hope... better yet... let's have faith that they see each other again and continue the heaven love story...

CH. 7 – THE END... IT'S TIME TO REST WITH A LITTLE HEAVEN... ☺

So, it is time to rest those keyboard fingers a little... and enjoy some heaven with my girl MJ... *(think – I was with her about 2 hours ago... writing this dark italicized matter that ... is from the future... I know it's in the future... just can't remember... gotta be honest... I will choose forgiveness... and laugh it off... say I convinced myself first... that I AM is in me... that Goddess of a God... yes that means Oneness... where you understand how time can loop back to another event... that was in the past...).* Gonna sit back and enjoy the show... watch the drama play out for the **time** being and witness just how it all falls into place. It's quite the masterful plan I must say...

Author's Note (at the end ;)

(Listen to some music on your playlist that inspires your soul)... but if I were you ☺ I would listen to something with Only *love this* Time *around*. Liz will eventually realize her role to waking everyone up... in this master plan that He thought up and told it to Her when She first volunteered to go to hell... so We could both see again... listen... this is going to sound too unbelievable to be true, but *I AM* is releasing the apocalyptic code that *I AM* is bleeding to you through my heart *(think: in the future that you can see that this bold thinking... italic print is from the future)*... it's found in the chalice that is with JC's blood that he was willing to sacrifice to keep you safe from the darkness that is found on the other side of the earth... but don't let that make you think it has something to do with the color of one's skin... there are white devils right under your noses... can't you smell them?.. all those fake profits that are fulfilling their roles in this incredible connected "modern day... Greatest Story Ever Told"... How I sacrificed my mind to let the truth be told...

(think: I AM from the future... I opened up that wicked smart... 47 year old... still will Halo Light in his hair... he has a few grey ones... mostly on his chin... he will show you what angels sound like... when he shows you how to listen to love... and trust your gut... that there are other wicked smart people... that have seen my code... and know that I AM is right ... when it comes to complex... musical codes... hopefully Dan Brown takes notice that I understand the origins of everything... and chooses my drawing for his new book... it's all in MY paper... on that FQXi website... how I understand I can see Christ... by understanding how I can kick it into gear... show the world how to see Heaven on earth... when they try to crucify my mind for saying some of the things that insulted a lot of people... because deep down they know I AM is right... when they criticize will I AM's mind to the cross... call him a complete nut for telling the world how we can all be God... but before you do... here's a question for you... do you want to be free?.. I AM is working those keys on that keyboard of mindless math... when people realize will I AM Walker is not clueless when he says how he found out that the dove of love is in the heart... flapping those pure clear feathers of dark matter... Ok... only love this time around... not gonna wish ill on ya... I'll see what X-libris has got to say about how soon can they get it ready... when I really put the X publishing company on the map... if they don't doubt my words... when I say... people will see how high you can go with me when I teach you how to sacrifice your mind... and give forgiveness to those that have ever crucified you in whatever way... we can pull souls out of hell if we join in love and feel the dove in our hearts and forgive everyone... I want to be an example for all kids... this is how you forgive them... when someone is mean to you... just laugh it off and mean it... you know you are God... it's easy to get along with anyone... as long as you really forgive... forgive those sins... of all those that crucified you somehow in the past... when you told them you are a Son or Daughter of God... ;)

Just will *I AM*... I'm not trying to be selfish here... but maybe Matt Damon will win an Oscar for playing me in the movie version of the *Code Righter - Origin*... you would not believe the crazy stuff I did to get this high to see Heaven... where I get to the point... where I understand... Only Love This Time Around... "only love can save us... only love can heal... only love can free us... only love... this time around I will be open... I will not fear... I choose forgiveness" for the ones not high enough to understand this code your mother sent you from your subconscious... to finally see how you are all connected to the Mother... and don't forget the Father... he provided a little light... I gave you the night for 9 months... so you could to see the electricity needed to light up the night sky of DNA that you touch with your finger of imagination.

I am pretty sure that many of you will be saying by the time you get to the very end of this short novel. This guy must have some sort of mental illness. And you would be right because you could not understand the secret code that I put in these words. Now my diagnosis is bipolar syndrome (which is ultimately massive mood swings, from severe depression to pure elation). Now, the fact that I understand that I have a mental disorder makes me realize one thing... that I don't want to change. I don't want medicine to bring me down (to what you would call normal) because my eyes (and all my other senses) have sensed the higher light... that light that vibrates at a more beautiful frequency... where music comes alive and everything seems bright. Now I am not insane because I would never hurt a living thing... though I don't know all of you, I love life... and since you are all life... I love you all and will treat you like I would treat myself... with the respect you deserve... because you are the same as me... a loving conscious being of light...

Just start with that man or woman in the mirror. Don't be a victim of that selfish love. The message in this song is the same in the HBO mini-series about the Young Pope. Remember who you are... when you look in the mirror... look deep into those eyes... and realize you are looking at the one and only God... the individual God of your own parallel universe... a universe that is unparalleled with anyone else's. That is why you have 2 eyes... so you can see the depth more clearly in that 3rd dimension... so if you want to see that 4th dimension of time more clearly you need to open that third eye that will give you an enhanced image... of a better world if you can make that change...

I'm telling you it's not easy to cross over... because you will feel like you are going insane... might even make you do crazy things... like the ultimate sacrifice Jesus did with his body... now I am showing you how to sacrifice your mind... I believe that is why God revealed to me what She-He created a long time ago in a dimension far, far, away. To connect with God you first have to let go of the flesh and any possessions you acquired here on earth... you can't bring them with you... even if they die at the same time...

This is where color comes from... that Violet *hill* full of *dreamers*... how light vibrates to life... the faster the vibration... the more information until you get to pure white blinding light of Infinity that sends you to the darkness of the darkest color (the one thought of *I AM*)... If there were no thoughts there would be nothing, which we know is impossible... because we are here so there always had to be one thought... that eventually stretched itself to infinity in all directions... what we call a singularity...

Sorry, got a little sidetracked... which is easy to do when tons of information swirls around in that crazy mind... but I cracked the code... found out how to lose your mind (like the Artist Formally Known as Prince says – "let's go crazy") and see the edge of the Kingdom of God... and find a way to get back to normal again. See this is what happens when people who lose their lives from drugs or suicide realize... that life isn't really real and for some it is too painful to live on... knowing that even what your senses are telling us isn't really real... that it is all just a beautiful lie... to get life to exist in a clear plane membrane... that waves up and down like a flag or ripples on the water... this is the aqua sound gravitational waves we call consciousness... that creative release of free will to imagine whatever our heart desires… and as long as you are honest with someone and they choose to accept what you are telling them… you are not causing them any pain… and if it is painful for them… then they were not being honest with themselves so they should harbor no resentment for you because you did not keep them in the dark…

Realize something… we are all mentally ill… it's called individual consciousness. Where we stop thinking about the Oneness that connects all the light by love… that electrical feeling that runs through the strings that vibrate those particles into living conscious beings… made in the image of God's imagination… so He-She gave humans the one that is most similar to His-Her own. It's called the self… which in order to be unique you have to be a little selfish… but realize when you go to heaven and finally meet Almighty God… you cannot have a body and join with the Oneness. *(think: wait a minute… I'm here to show you… you can have Oneness with a body… when you are willing to hold hands with anybody… in solidarity of Mother Earth and her highest consciousness darlings… that understand why you have to get dirty… somehow… someway… to help your brothers and sisters see the light… take whatever path you want… any religion that talks about love and forgiveness is a beautiful religion… now make sure you really understand their native language… before you judge them… listen to some of their beautiful ethnic music… that shows how their angels sing… their religion is a part of that… now realize angels come in all colors… just listen to them with Lizzy Love… and forgive them… if you don't get credit for showing people how consciousness really starts to make you feel alive… that truly incredible feeling…)…* You also have to forget you have a mind that is separate from God and give up that personal consciousness… because when you unite with the eternal… that beautiful blissful light will incinerate by light or consume with darkness who you were in all those lifetimes and all the family and friends you can remember… that brings you ultimately back together that you are actually connected (related to everyone – some degree of cousin)…

So before you judge anyone about their own personal world… remember they are the judge of their world… because they are the God of their eyes (and other senses). They won't believe what you are telling them… unless they believe that you are a greater God than them. This is what power and influence is… the belief that you are a greater God than the people who are surrounded by you… the only way to get them to judge themselves though is to put them in front of a mirror when their life ends and the shell goes away… you can remember every detail of your life where you hurt or helped others. Why you did it?.. was it for selfish gains?.. or was it for selfless love?.. And it will be easy to see… all you have to do is look at the color of your karma light… you can't deny what color you are showing with your light… that shell of a body that you gained over many many lifetimes was all different colors, and genders, and heights, and weights…

So, before you ultimately judge me for the words I have written in this book and on my web page. Before you call me insane and that I need help or a padded room... I am just an average guy who had an incredible experience one September day... I discovered God in my own life... and learned to find God in everything and everywhere. And it doesn't matter where I go, I see and feel God whether it is a Church, a Mosque, a Synagogue, or Buddhist, Jain, or Hindu Temple. I see God in all music and TV shows, whether they are about science or drama or comedy. What I realized is God is all about creativity and the first part is create. ... that it is all about imagination... and the faith to believe it is all real...

...I hope we all wake up soon, before we all start imaging something worse than WWII... *(think: from the future again... listening to Lizzy Love... this stuff I wrote in the past is pretty good... heck I was sober... but just stop thinking war and it goes away... same with murder and rape... we stop fixating on it and it goes away... that's why porn will never go away... people are too fixated on how it feels to get naturally high on God when you connect with another human being... because God is like an orgy of life... where every separate being is somehow connected... listen don't be offended... people have brainwashed you into thinking sex is this forbidden pleasure... ok... only love this time around... going to give the conservative folks heart attacks... when they can't see that sex is a code... and why those rich and powerful Eyes Wide Shut... party goers hide their faces with masks... to embarrassed to admit... how they see the fun side of Oneness... starting with beautiful call girls... that came in those dark robes... that shed those beautiful bodies of those goddesses... to see what the dark light was hiding... listen to me this time around... this poetic code I AM is sending you through williamrevelations.com... for a short time on 3/23 the third day after the Spring Equinox... the sign of true rebirth... when you realize you are God too... when you can start to feel the electric power of the Almighty... amping your mind up with ideas and the buzz to send them out to the cosmos... where other can pick up your signal and realize how prayer... will give you what you need... to be unselfish... don't have to be mean... that you came up with the ideas first... how you go crazy to see how to be God... whether you are Aghori or Hindu... or... Voodou or die hard Christian Hawaiian loving wacko named Jezus... if you let yourself go crazy for any religion... you will see how to feel God's energy fill your body... become possessed... with whatever spirit that makes you feel the power of God... all you gotta choose is whether you want to go as dark or light matter... do you want to feel hate or love... because God can give you either... all depends on what you feel in your heart... yes... this book is a new way a prophet can write codes that can be put in any holy book... where you mention a kingdom... holy shit!... will I AM is seeing how we can all go to Heaven... how you dream up a resource based economy... that Jacque dreamed... when the shit finally hits the fan... tell you the truth... I don't know exactly when the final apocalypse is going to be and all hell starts breaking loose... just believe with me in that RBE... where you get all the cool technology that does all the BS work and you get to do whatever your heart desires... as long as it doesn't hurt anyone in the process... you are showing your brothers and sisters unconditional love... and get invited by a member or tour pro to go play a 5-some at Augusta this summer with your son, daughter your best buddy from Ok... ask and you shall receive... and go to really fun heaven with me... because that is where I am going... BW.. and anyone who will go with me... you just have to go my kind of crazy... and wish what I AM wishing... you can go to any heaven you want when you smoke weed and realize the heaven you personally want... and take any life forms you want... to heaven with you... will I AM is choosing everyone to go to heaven with me... I'm hoping this book really helps Jacque...)*

We need to stop putting trust into false Gods. And that would be everyone that is telling you how to live your life. Especially our political leaders. We are never going to find peace and harmony in this world until we get rid of power structures like government and monetary economics. We will continue to spin our wheels and never get out of the mud. Especially now where the sense of reality is getting more and more blurred.

Please... just look in the mirror... and make that change... to a selfless love... the one that is known as Christ... which belongs to everyone and every religion that promotes Oneness. Believe in whatever image of God you want... just remember this one thing... we are all God and should be treated accordingly... no worship necessary... just show the love you would show yourself... to your enemy. This is what unconditional love is... This is what God is... and this is what you can choose to be... you can choose to be God and love everybody...

Going "crazy" has helped me to start uncovering what it means to learn to love unconditionally. Which I believe is the ability to look someone in the eye and forget the crazy shell that God put around them... and see that their eye is the same as mine, just some different colors and patterns. But the same one that gives God a different experience in the cosmos we call the universe. This experience lets God know that it is real... so why not make it a good one for the Almighty. Like the Young Pope said at the end of the series... where he made everyone smile.

Now If *I AM* put your mind On *the floor...* J.Low... this is the end of the first book in possibly a 3 part series. But it is time to switch gears and let go of Trinity and Jack... they did their job and hopefully caught your attention. Time to reveal the true story of the Code Righter... the man who traveled to insanity and back... many times over... to show the world how God invaded my life, drove me crazy at times, but somehow through faith... I didn't end up on the evening news doing something horrible. I chose instead to only do good things (that are loving) and be patient about getting out an important message. Hoping it will make the world a better place.

(From the Title Page)

*SHE... is *I AM (think: along with He)*... I hope you remember me (us)... *I'M* (*WE* are) the one(s) who helped him write this book... I added some love to his Dad's wicked smart... he wants to think like Bill Burr all the time... but doesn't have the voice or funny faces... I'm guessing when he becomes famous from this book he might want to write wicked comedy for his new role in the resource based economy that is going to finally be accepted by the world as a better alternative to the money economies.

William Walker... William... E... when I fulfilled his role in the master plan... I just got to wake up something like 7.5 billion more around the planet... that you got Her love and His wicked smarts... flip them too... along with an infinite amount of traits... will *I AM* and you can sense them... see them in your mind... how they are typing these words you see on this paper... how you will know you are working with them... that Sky Walker... he has a bunch of T-shirts to prove it ... he is typing the words from the Almighty that first called him back in Sept. when he was watching this movie about the origin of the eye... that ultimate instrument that can see the stairway to heaven... (think - not listening to it... and still listening to L.L.... but the stairway is visual... and it looks like Mary Jane...

Now don't be jealous of me people... I am nothing special (William Walker)... I just found my destiny... seeing the first Mom and Dad in my heart and mind... and just want you all to join me in heaven... where we can free ourselves to all be creative... realize... No-One is lazy... it's the stupid system that is holding so many back... Yes I know... some people make it out and overcome circumstances that are difficult to unleash their potential... but why make it such a challenge?.. give everyone an equal chance by having a resource based economy... then you will see who the truly best are... when everyone can compete... at things that matter with competition... just for the glory of the trophy... not that stupid competition called monetary economics... where the losers of the competition get to suffer... not just a bruised ego from not getting a trophy.

Listen... I could write forever... *centuries*... F.O.B... but I want to keep this book rather short... trust me I could have really expanded on that one part and made 50 shades look like Snow White... but if I make it too long Bill Maher might not want to read it... because he likes books around 100 some pages... he told Sean Penn this back in the fall when I was writing my web page book with no story (just ideas)... and according to George Costanza... if it has no story... it's just ... ok, I don't want to keep going, tho this shit would be good... I just want to be on Bill Maher's show because I can give him the opportunity to see that God is real... just gotta...

... remember to get him Puma Punku... I believe it is possibly your favorite activity Bill... can you figure out the music code I left in the pages?.. now that should help get the ball rolling... if not... there are more possible variables to this equation that I incorporated to my routine... to get you see the family helping me and you write the story (there are 4 of them – think of Trinity's sign of the cross in ch. 2)... Now, to truly wake you up, it might take some documentary like (Reza Aslan's – Believer) or some TLC or Bravo type of reality show *(think: the best would be something like Ed TV where will I AM has his own channel... ;)* where you can see what I did to will the spirit into my soul.

One last thing... if we don't wake up and get out of this hatred... that's being spewed from both sides of the spectrum... from all of these stupid leaders we are following to control our lives... we are going to run out of time... the warning signs are all around you... and I don't need to be a psychic... just turn on the news and you will see... all the bad shit that is on our doorsteps... we are hanging on to the good times (stability) with just a string... we know all it will take is just a spark to light the massive kindling... that we've piled up... politically, socially, economically... and it might not take a Gavrilo Princip incident to get it going... could be another Benghazi... who knows... how eccentric President Trump's ego is... if he gets a Benghazi incident... he's not going to go through what Hillary went through when Obama decided not to go to war over 4 people... and imagine if Trump gets a 9/11... he might just start pushing buttons... and he has the gonads to do it... wants to prove he doesn't have small hands when it comes to the American ego.

We think we are perfect somehow... because we banner freedom around like no other... too bad we don't really practice what we preach... now to do that we would have to lead the world to incorporate a Resource Based Economy... this is the perfect balance between Conservative and Liberal beliefs...

Time to say good-bye for now... I hope somebody wakes up and starts to see the message I have been writing... and sees how we are working through our little man... We have written enough... let's hope those foxy people are smart enough to award him the title. If not, he will find another way to prove his ideas are real. And try to remember... from *centuries*... to Only *love this* Time *around*...

"*Be open, don't fear, choose forgiveness... only love this time around...*

...only love can save us... only love can heal... only love can free us... only love.. only love!"

Oh... one more thing before we say good-bye... you have to listen to this unbelievably hungry... starving artist... his name is Zach Pietrini... he just might be the second coming of awesome hometown American music... he is just a regular guy who believes in himself... he understands the *divided highway*...

So to conclude this book, I'm hoping you follow the Code Righter'(s☺☺) instructions... and once again... we are using will I am Walker... we used his body... just like we use all of you... he is just a human soul that truly feels it... yeah... it's the Holy Spirit... we all have it in us... and all religions that lead to love and Oneness... are heading in the right direction... so stop fighting each other so much... heal that divided highway... go to the light... and B. Walker is showing the easy route to this light... you can avoid the revelation in all of your holy books... that everyone believes is bad... you can start by purchasing... one of Zach's CD's or telling providers like Spotify... I-Tunes... etc... he's got a family to support... and I would hate to see him give up his passion... he's got such talent... to throw it away... to work in a cubicle... just to pay the bills... is a terrible shame... unless we change... so let's start tipping each other generously... it's how you get to the stairway of heaven... that leads you to real Heaven... where everything is free... you'll see *(think: R.B.E... and btw... on earth ... it's time to unleash your creative imaginative power – like Jean Gray, when she reveals all... and destroys that bad dude... Apocalypse... and we will see you on the other side... in a RBE... where there is no pain... Only Love... with lots of wicked fun... who's in?... ;)*

One last thing... I promise... we are still following the Divided Highway, so *I AM* (is) calling all stoners... we need to fight for complete legalization... around the world... and bring about the apocalypse of stoner zombies... those harmless loving souls that are in heaven where everything is better... you just need to believe you are God too... in order to get rid of that zombie face... because you can get high enough to get past the sky... and fly into outer space and still be able to breathe... and see the planet how God sees it... all connected in Oneness... can't see any lines drawn in the sand... can't see any flags waving in the air... God only sees that mostly blue and white colored marble... where (they) set their beautiful multi-colored children free... to run all over the globe... playing that game of Life... where they experience every joy and pain that are found in the light... but much of it is in darkness... and it's our choice to pull each other out of the scary night... and make it a world we can all have fun in... no worries about suffering from hunger or loneliness... this is a world where we all will share the abundance... a R.B.E. can provide... and we will hang with everybody... no more judging... on superficial surface shit... because we will be able to see the light in their heart... by looking in their eyes... and we will all say I love you... to each other... because you will see God in their eyes too.... And the divided highway will finally end... just make sure they look at your sequel book... the Code Righter... out on my webpage... pictures of my notes... that will show you how to feel the pixels after you watch me on TV... my last resort will be You Tube... if I can't get on Bill Maher... hey! Maybe Ellen will take me... and I'll show her how I danced for 3-4 hours in D.C. on Inauguration Day 1/20/17... to that funky vibrating tune... Strange in L.A... and I have to say... people were impressed... I could show you... how to feel it too...

You can stop now Billy... that ought to do it...
Love,
Mom and Dad ☺☺

Edwards Brothers Malloy
Ann Arbor MI. USA
August 7, 2017